UNVEILED
MEMORIES

IDA PALUCH KERSZ

IPK Books

Wilmette, Illinois

Unveiled Memories © 2019 Ida Paluch Kersz
ISBN-13: 978-0-578-59227-5

This book is a memoir. I have tried to recreate events, locales and conversations from my memories of them. In order to maintain their anonymity in some instances I have changed the names of individuals and places, I may have changed some identifying characteristics and details such as physical properties, occupations and places of residence.

Edited by Zelda Marbell Fuksman

I would like to thank Danny Spungen and the Florence and Laurence Spungen Family Foundation for all of their assistance in bringing my story to publication. I appreciate their help more than I can say.

Cover design by Phil Velikan

Packaged by Wish Publishing

Printed in the United States of America
10 9 8 7 6 5 4 3 2 1

UNVEILED MEMORIES

ACKNOWLEDGEMENTS

For many years I lived my life with a hole in my soul that could not be filled. Something was missing. In 1995 my beating heart found its echo – the heartbeat of my twin brother, Adam. Each of our questioning and seeking finally came to an end when we met and confirmed that our search was over—we belonged together. I am finally free to share my struggles and my story, which from tragedy turned to joy.

After many long years and resolving many issues, I am now able to share and publish my life. It is not to applaud me but to validate a history that was only a mirage at times. Many children were saved by good people who discovered their identity after their adopted parents passed on.

I want to thank Zelda Marbell Fuksman who came into my life during the gathering of the Holocaust Association of Child Survivors (HACS) in Skokie. She gave me strength to speak and to take a chance to confirm my dream of reuniting with my twin. Her kindness to edit my story was not only helpful, but she, as a child survivor, was able to see through my eyes and feel my heart, my fears, and joys. She understood and validated my life.

My dear daughter Ester has been my treasure that helped me salvage my life with dignity and supported my search to find the missing pieces of my life.

I am grateful that I have a brother. Adam has added and validated my memories, my need to be connected to my twin. I am proud of the man that he is and appreciate his sons and grandchildren.

Also, my special friend Carol Simon is my inspiration at the Illinois Holocaust Museum and Education Center in Skokie.

Thank you, Danny, an angel who gave me important help when I needed it. Words can't describe my gratitude for this wonderful friend. I also have to mention his sweet wife, Natalie, who supported his decision. I feel so very lucky to have them in my life.

I must acknowledge, in memoriam, my dearest Polish mother Jozefa Maj. She taught me how to love.

And a special thanks to a special lady, Merle R. Saferstein, for the additional copy-editing of the final manuscript.

INTRODUCTION

A frightful scene tortured my mind and crowded my memory, which I could not understand or give a meaning to. As a child of only three years, I could not name my fears or loss. All I knew was that my whole life changed that one day.

As I grew older, the scenes and memories were veiled—they seemed like a nightmare. With time and maturity, I came to realize the truth and the tragedy that befell me, my family, and the Jewish people.

This is my story. A story of a child survivor—a hidden child who had to reestablish her identity and her family and save memories full of suffering, tears, and th e acceptance of many identities. My confused mind had to endure and bend with all situations and yet find a way to save myself. There must have been a bigger purpose to my life. I had to relearn my history and connection to my family, especially the inner longing for my twin brother. Our adult family gave him up for lost, but my inner soul never let go of the echo of my twin's heartbeat.

This book, my story, speaks of a child who learned to revive her own soul and identify a missing link through a constant state of questioning and searching. Even during my very young years, I had something unresolved gnawing at my inner self, giving me strength to rebuild, heal, and seek to recapture a connection, daring to be bold.

I share with you my little stories of how and what it took to capture the adult I had to become. Some of my accounts of play, school, the dreams and hopes of a child going through the stages may seem simple or trivial, but just as children under normal circumstances of reaching adulthood go through stages, so did I but in a much faster and dramatic way. I learned how to survive as a Catholic, a Jew, a Communist child, a Zionist, and an American with liberties and freedoms to speak, share, and advance kindness as a good human being, accepting of all people.

1

MY FAMILY

My family had an interesting history, which was not part of my young years because of the circumstances of my survival. After I was returned to my Jewish roots, I learned about them, their lives, and their struggles.

My father, Chaim Leizer Paluch, (Polish first name Leon), came looking for work to the big city of Sosnowiec from the small town of Zarnowiec in his mid-teens. He apprenticed as a tailor and lived in the tailor's home, as was done in those times. The first years of the apprenticeship did not include tailoring, rather he was used as a servant, performing household chores and caring for the family's little children.

My mother, Ester Wajntraub, came from a little town Szczekociny, where her father, Moishe Yidel Wajntraub, managed a large flour mill for a Polish nobleman. Grandfather provided for their needs and kept his large family together. Moishe and Grandmother Ryvka Wellner Wajntraub, raised a family of thirteen children, eight girls and five boys. They were a close-knit family and were well-regarded and admired for their beauty.

When the girls were dressed in their finery for the holidays, Grandmother Ryvka accompanied them to the door and *sheped nachas* (gloried with pleasure) as she gazed after them walking down the street until they disappeared from sight. She raised her arms to heaven blessing them for a safe outing.

Just as she was religious, she also was an avid Zionist and did not hesitate to champion her strong opinions to whoever would listen. When Grandfather died suddenly of an unknown illness, the family fell on hard times. All the children were forced to move to larger cities to earn a living for themselves. The two oldest sons left Poland, possibly to South Africa, and all contact was lost.

My mother, Ester, was an attractive girl whose beauty was enhanced by her glowing complexion and distinctive, expressive, green eyes. Her braided, light brown hair, set like a crown on her head, gave her a regal appearance. Mother was a modest girl and followed the customs of the religious observances. She moved to Sosnowiec, a coal-mining city of Poland, where she worked in a store as a sales girl and struggled to maintain a living.

Not having a dowry to attract a good match, it was difficult to get married, so when her sister Zosia introduced her to my father, who was a widower with a little son, Mother accepted this match. She was twenty- two years old, which was considered quite old for those times. They settled in the suburb of Pogon and led a happy, good life. They managed to earn a living by Father sewing clothing items and Mother selling them at a market.

In 1929, my parents were blessed with a daughter Gienia, Jewish name Gitele, whose kind and sweet demeanor was cherished and admired. My twin Adam and I were born on May 3, 1939, the anniversary of the Polish constitution. Mother thought she was expecting one baby but was actually carrying triplets. Sometime during the pregnancy, she had a miscarriage and did not realize that she was still pregnant. A few weeks later when she felt life inside her, the doctor confirmed that indeed she was carrying a baby.

When the time of delivery came, my brother Adam was born first, healthy and noisy, and to everyone's surprise, a fraternal twin followed. I came out five minutes later, a lifeless, blue baby.

The doctor asked Mother if she wished to save the baby girl. My mother cried hysterically and begged the doctor to do everything

Gienia With Mother And Father, circa 1935

possible.On September 1, 1939, three months after my brother and I were born, World War II broke out. Father, a dedicated citizen, joined the Polish Army to defend our country. Mother was left with three children— two of them infants.

Mother continued, with difficulty, selling clothing at the market, while my ten-year-old sister Gienia helped with the care of the house and of my brother and me. Her innocent childhood was cut short.

Gienia was a beautiful child with shiny, dark hair and bright, blue eyes, like Father's. Whenever she managed to get a little free time from her responsibilities, she joined the neighborhood children in play and usually was the leader. She was a feisty girl, which was a helpful trait during the Nazi occupation in managing to talk her way through the long lines for bread.

2

SOSNOWIEC

Before the war, there were about 30,000 Jews in Sosnowiec, making up about twenty percent of the town's population. The city was taken over by the Germans on the first day of invasion of Poland. Arrests and beatings of prominent Jews began. On September 9, 1939, the Great Synagogue in Sosnowiec was burned.

Local Jews were being evicted from better homes and terrorized by the locals on the streets. Jewish businesses were looted. Shortly after the first mass executions followed. Jews had to relocate into overcrowded tenements, and the ghetto was created. In the next couple of years, thousands of Jews were relocated to Sosnowiec from the smaller towns. The Jewish population grew to 45,000.

A Judenrat and Jewish police were organized, as ordered by the occupiers. The head of the Judenrat was Moshe Merin. Food rationing began. The Jews were not allowed to buy anything outside their own community.

A labor camp was formed for the deportees from Czechoslovakia to work at the Shine Brothers factory. Many labor factories were established for the locals; making uniforms, underwear, corsets, bags, leather handbags, and military boots. By 1942, over 10,000 profiteers established slave labor factories. In addition deportations were occurring, organized by the Germans with the help of the Judenrat and Merin, selecting healthy men for slave labor at the camps. Large transfers of Jews took place in May and June of 1942.

Between October 1942 to January 1943, the ghetto was moved to the Serodula district. At this point about 13,000 Jews still lived in Sosnowiec. The creation of the Sosnowiec ghetto was completed on March 10,1943, when it was finally closed off from the outside world.

The deportation of Jews from the Sosnowiec Ghetto, circa 1942

Thousands of Jews were deported from Sosnowiec to Auschwitz in June 1943 during the major deportation action. The ghetto was liquidated two months later in August. The remaining Jews were deported to Auschwitz. A few hundred Jews remained in the Serodula ghetto, which was liquidated in January 1944.

3

THE NIGHTMARE BEGINS

In 1942, the Nazis moved the Jewish population of about 28,000 into the ghetto in the downtown area. Some were from Sosnowiec, and a multitude were from the surrounding towns, which were densely populated with Jewish people. Later, in 1943, they were moved into a smaller ghetto Srodula. Soon after, they began selections. Jews were rounded up and terrorized—first mass executions followed by forced relocations.

One day, on August 14, 1942, the scene of my nightmare began. I was three-years old. My family was among the throng gathered in a selection line to be taken away to be killed. I could not understand what was happening. The distress and complete chaos impacted terror in every face, as I saw the crowds screaming and running in different directions.

I was trying to cling to the figure of my mother running at the head of the crowd, along with my twin brother, Adam, and older sister, Gienia. As we tried to keep up with her, Mother ran into a building and up a wooden staircase. She seemed to be driven senseless, without any concern for her little children running behind her. She ran to the second floor and into a closet, but this did not seem where she intended to go. She continued her frantic run up another set of stairs, climbed up to a window, and disappeared from sight. Sometime later, I saw her lifeless body outside. This desperate and disturbed act of Mother's suicide disrupted the Gestapo's plan. They canceled the selection for the day, not wanting to incite further rioting.

Mother's sister Rozia and her children were with us in the ghetto when my Mother's suicide disrupted the selection. It caused people to scurry into hiding places. It also gave Aunt Rozia the opportunity to snatch us away and hurry us from the grim sight of Mother's death.

A few weeks later, Wilhelm Maj, who had been a produce supplier to my aunt's fruit store, came from Czestochowa looking for her at her apartment. The neighbors told him to look in the ghetto. He loitered near the barbed wire fence, which surrounded the ghetto, and spotted Aunt Rozia and me walking nearby. Wilhelm called her over and asked who was the child she was holding by the hand.

"This child is my sister's, who committed suicide and is one mouth too many to feed," she replied.

Wilhelm's face and countenance were affected as he looked at the innocent blond toddler clinging to Rozia. He offered to take me with him on the condition that I must remain with him forever and that no claim would be made to return me in the future. Aunt Rozia knew that this was my only chance to survive (Aunt Rozia and her family were murdered).

In the dusk of the dwindling daylight, Aunt Rozia handed me over the barbed wires to this man. His strong, warm arms sheltered me as he carried me home to his wife Jozefa, in the city of Czestochowa, which means "often hides." This became my new home and family. It was the last time I ever saw my twin brother, Adam, sister, Gienia, and the extended family.

Czestochowa is a major city in southern Poland on the Warta River—one of the largest in Poland. It is known for the famous Pauline Monastery of Jasna Góra, which is the home of the Black Madonna painting/icon (*Jasnogórski Cudowny obraz Najœwiêtszej Maryi Panny Niepokalanie Poczêtej*)— a shrine to the Virgin Mary.

We arrived at Wilhelm's home on Christmas Eve of 1942. As he handed me over to his wife, Jozefa, he said, "Here is your Christmas gift." Jozefa looked at me tenderly, embraced me, and instantly accepted me as her child, even though she was three months pregnant. They both knew that death was the punishment for hiding a Jew.

I was told by Mother Jozefa that when Wilhelm brought me to their home, I spoke only Yiddish. I cried bitterly and wanted to go back to my brother and sister. They had to hide me for weeks and teach me to answer in Polish and especially to recite prayers in Polish.

The evening that I was brought to my Polish parents, I woke up in the middle of the night and observed my new family decorating a Christmas tree. Wilhelm was dressed in a Santa Claus suit, but he did not fool me, I still called him Daddy, as I was told it was his name.

A few weeks later, I remember being dressed in a beautiful long white dress and brought to a spacious church where everything smelled new and unusual to me. A priest was speaking in a strange language, which I could not understand, while he splashed water on my head. After this ceremony, I was called Irena Maj, with a new Christian birth certificate dated January 3, 1942.

My new parents told their priest, the one who baptized me, that I was their own illegitimate child, and that until now they kept me hidden in a village until they got married. This fact was told to all their relations, friends, and neighbors, and the truth was never disclosed. My oppressive, starving ghetto, surroundings, and past life melted away from my memory. Now I had a new family. A mother, Jozefa Maj, (maiden name Domanska) and a daddy, Wilhelm Maj. My new parents indulged all my wishes and needs without hesitation and with love. Their laps were always a welcome, warm retreat. I was completely absorbed into their lives and community. We lived in a two-family house with a welcoming backyard, where I rode my tricycle and played with the local children.

Daddy Wilhelm earned a living selling cigarettes and vodka to the neighboring towns and villages, traveling there with a horse and wagon. He used to travel with two companions, Franciszek and Leon Mlek.

On February 11, 1943, Daddy, with his companions, went to the village of Odorz with a wagon filled with illegal merchandise. The three were apprehended by the Gestapo and were executed   on the spot.

My Polish mother Jozefa and father Wilhelm Maj, circa 1935

Witnesses told Jozefa that before her husband was shot, he lamented what would happen to his beloved wife Jozefa and daughter Irena.

I remember the dreary, cold, snowy, winter day as we transported Wilhelm's body in a horse-drawn wagon on an icy road. Our little group was followed by mourners. Jozefa's mother-in-law, who became my grandmother, and I were petrified, screaming as Grandfather whipped the horses mercilessly in his drunken state. Daddy Wilhelm and his companions were laid to rest next to each other in the Czestochowa cemetery. Later, Grandpa built a big family monument with a picture of the young man on a porcelain plaque, which was placed above a poem inscribed in the stone. The poem read, "*Spij tatusiu ukochany juz sie nigdty nie zobaczysz ze swoimi coreczkami.*" (Sleep beloved Father. You won't see your daughters ever again.)

After Wilhelm's death, Mother and Grandmother always dressed in black. They wore hats with black veils covering their faces. Mother made me a black band to wear on my coat sleeve. Our life took on a cheerless and dark existence. No one laughed anymore. A few months

Memorial monument for my Polish father Wilhelm Maj. The litle children on the right are Ida and Wilusia, 1946.

later, Jozefa delivered a baby girl who was named Wilusia after her deceased father Wilhelm.

Jozefa, a daughter of a poor, widowed dressmaker, had married Wilhelm, her high school sweetheart, without the blessing of his parents. This connection was unacceptable to Wilhelm's father, Grandpa Maj, who had been an officer in the Russian Czar's Army before the Russian Revolution. Later, when the Communists took over power of Russia, he and his family fled to Poland as refugees.

Wilhelm was their only son and heir to their wealth, which they managed to bring with them from Communist Russia. After his son's marriage to Jozefa, Grandpa never included Wilhelm in his family business and disowned him after learning of his elopement.

Grandpa Maj was involved in many businesses. One was a coal warehouse, selling coal to the community. The warehouse and a stable where he housed a few horses were attached to the right wing of the apartment building where we lived. In addition to the coal business,

Grandpa Wladyslaw Maj in the Czar's army, circa 1916.

Wladyslaw, Wilhelm and Jozefa Maj in Czarist Russia, 1907.

Grandmother Jozefa and Wilhelm in
Russia before the Revolution, 1912.

he also had a taxi service transporting people around town in horse-drawn carriages.

On many occasions, I observed and was intrigued by the array and display of wagons used for different occasions, especially funerals. A special black funeral carriage was decorated like a large glass cage, with lacquered edges and gold filigree designs to add dignity and importance to the occasion. The casket was placed inside and was surrounded by colorful flowers for all to see as it was transported to the cemetery. The carriage was pulled by one or sometimes more horses.

Another carriage, used for weddings, was embellished with a white leather convertible top, usually decorated with flowers, white ribbons, and green garlands. After a while, funerals and weddings became less festive. More and more funerals were held in secret so as not to offend the local German Gestapo who were responsible for most of the deaths. Grandpa's other enterprises were a billiard room with a restaurant and a laundry with a *magiel*, where linens were pressed with large wooden rollers.

With the loss of his only son, Grandpa showed his guilt by displays of anger and uncontrolled frenzies. He became an alcoholic and his violent behavior threatened all of us. Grandpa Maj frequently cursed his own wife, Grandma Jozefa, who had the same name as my Polish mother, by calling her names like *kurwa twoja mac*, (Your mother was a whore), and often kicked her legs, which resulted in infected wounds that remained open and would not heal.

Mother, with a new baby, Wilusia, and no income, had to move in with Grandma Jozefa and Grandpa Wladyslaw into their three-room apartment, which was located on the ground level at Katedralna 14. It was not an ideal shelter from our struggling lives.

The place was small and presented frightening surroundings, especially for a young child. I was terrified of the living room where three stuffed deer heads with glass eyes hung on the walls. The sparkling eyes stared and followed me no matter how I tried to avoid their piercing looks. The room also boasted a huge grandfather clock

Ida, Grandmother Jozefa and baby Wilusia, 1943.

that chimed every hour, which made me jump until I got used to its vibrating ringing.

The grandparents shared their bedroom with me, where a small cot was placed against a wall. Here, too, a furry skin of a white bear with a stuffed head and glass eyes kept watch over me. These animals were the trophies from the good old days when Grandfather hunted. Mother Jozefa and I were also affected by Grandfather's raucous, mean behavior. He was in a constant rage and expressed it by tearing up the apartment. He broke dishes from the china cabinet, broke furniture and threw the pieces at us, while shouting swear words. He chased me with a whip made of a rabbit's foot and long strips of leather. When he hit me, he said, "Now you know who is the boss."

Sometimes I would hide in the clock, which had a cabinet large enough for me to sit with my knees under my chin. I shivered with fear and prayed to God to save us from any harm at the hands of the intoxicated grandfather.

Ida, Grandmother Jozefa and baby Wilusia, 1943.

Many times, we ran in the cold winter nights to the yard in our nightgowns just to get away from the wild, uncontrollable man. Morning after morning, half-asleep and still wearing only his long-john underwear, he swayed across the street to buy a new supply of alcohol. He then continued drinking until he was completely exhausted from his howls and chasing everyone around. The nightmare wouldn't end for the family until he finally passed out on his bed, usually in a pool of his own urine. It came to a point that Grandpa fed alcohol to his horses, the German shepherd dog, and even poured it into the canary's water container.

The neighbors heard his yelling but no one got involved. The only safe place was in Wilusias's crib—he left her alone. Out of desperation, and to escape her misery, Mother also started to drink in order to face the horrible situation we were in and try to stay sane.

To take me away from Grandfather's violence and to earn a living, Jozefa decided to take me along on the trains, where she sold merchandise out of suitcases. My being with her helped her sell things because people had compassion for a woman with a small child.

We sold tobacco. From cigarette butts that we found on the street, we retrieved small amounts of tobacco, which we reused. I learned to roll cigarettes in tissue paper. Home-made vodka was also a good seller. Jozefa poured the vodka into old alcohol bottles that we collected in the streets. She washed them and then applied a brown wax seal on top of the cork and pressed in the image of a *grosz*, (a small coin) to make it look authentic.

When she ran out of real vodka, she filled the bottles with half water and half alcohol and passed it off as one hundred percent alcohol. For this reason, we often changed our train routes in order to avoid being recognized as cheaters.

The trains were always packed. At every stop, the Gestapo came around looking for suspicious people. Mostly they were looking for Jews or contraband smugglers. They took pleasure intimidating the people to keep them scared.

On one of our escapades, Mother and I were separated when she stepped off the train first. I was not able to get off fast enough as the train was already moving, and the doors shut. I began to cry louder and louder until the conductor came, and took me to his home at the end of the trip. I cried and screamed, not wanting to eat or talk to anyone.

As Mother told me later, when she noticed that I was not near her, she immediately went to the train manager's office begging him to look for me. He was a sympathetic person, because the next day we were reunited, thanks to the people who helped us find each other. Mother rewarded everyone in the train manager's office with free cigarettes.

Often, when we traveled on the train, we had to sleep over in strangers' homes in different cities. It was not unusual for people, who lived close to train stations, to house travelers for the night for a fee. I used to sleep in a bed or on the floor with other children lined up like sardines, head to feet to head.

What stands out most and brings back apprehension and fear to this day were the sentry booths painted with stripes, where German soldiers stood guard all over the city. Other soldiers patrolled the streets with ferocious German shepherd dogs.

On our travels, our papers were demanded constantly. We saw many arrested and dragged off to the Gestapo headquarters. One unlucky trip took us to the Gestapo headquarters in our city of Czestochowa. We were coming home on a train on which the Gestapo were looking through peoples' luggage, pointing to the ones they wanted to be opened. When they pointed to our suitcase, I volunteered to open it, while Mother pretended that she did not hear the order, but the soldier persisted. At age five, I did not know the consequences.

When I opened the suitcase, he discovered cigarettes. We were arrested and taken off the train to headquarters and held in different rooms for interrogation. I found myself with a uniformed Gestapo man sitting behind a desk. I was scared and looked around for some sort of escape or comfort. My eyes stopped on a family picture on his desk, which also brought his attention to it. He stared at me with what seemed kind eyes, picked up the telephone, and spoke to someone in German. Soon I found myself running in the hallway into Mother's arms.

Our suitcase was returned with a warning in broken Polish by the officer speaking sternly, "Don't do it again. I have a little daughter like you, but someone else won't be as generous as I am, so don't let us see you again!"

Unfortunately, we could not comply with his warning. How else would we survive? Life in those days was full of dark secrets, dark skies, and dark apartments. At night we were awakened by squealing sirens warning the population of air raids, which forced a fearful run for cover to the basements. Everyone had to cover the windows at night with dark blankets to prevent any light peeking through to the outside so not to be a guide for bombers to drop their bombs. We had no electricity. Kerosene lamps, that gave off a smelly smoke, supplied the only dim light.

Hunger was constant. Mother started to sell furniture, clothing, and jewelry in order to keep us alive. She invented a flour soup that we ate cold and called white borscht. It was made of a cup of water and a spoonful of sourdough, which was made by leaving rye flour to stand for a day to ferment. Mother always was caring and made sure that the food and bread was divided fairly and evenly between her children and herself.

During those trying times, I remember being sick quite often, although I never saw a doctor. One of my ailments was whooping cough. Mother ran to the neighbor's in a panic for help when blood was pouring out of my nose, and I was choking. She bundled me up in warm clothing and a blanket, settled me in the small garden outside our house, and hoped that the sunshine would be a cure and would help me regain a healthy color.

As the war dragged on, our hunger and suffering increased. On many occasions, out of desperation, we searched through the neighbors' garbage looking for potato peels to cook for ourselves. When there was no food at all, Mother would say to Wilusia and me, "Go to sleep. Maybe you will forget that you are hungry."

But to sleep through the night was impossible. The bed bugs kept us awake to the point of desperation. It prompted us to get up in the middle of the night and shake the mattresses in the hope of loosening the bloodthirsty parasites. Mother would boil hot water and pour it on the slats and mattress to dislodge and kill the unwelcome, torturous bugs. I will never forget the foul smell of the dead bedbugs.

These were not the only pests that added to our suffering life and trials. Lice were constant companions, day and night. Our hair and bodies were their feeding source as they sucked our blood. They were in the hair and in every seam and fold of clothing. We spent hours looking for lice in each others' hair. Somehow this pastime was very reassuring and pleasant. I learned to kill them and to remove the eggs by squeezing each hair between my nails and pulling down in hopes of dislodging the clinging next generation of tiny pests.

Mother's tragedy of losing a husband and being the sole provider and caregiver of two little girls made her turn more and more to the only source of relief she knew - vodka. It also got her in trouble as she began keeping company with strange men. I remember one man who became Mother's lover. He worked for the fire department of the city. He was an alcoholic, and when Mother wasn't around, he would hold me with one hand and beat me with the other.

When we visited Mother's girlfriend who lived across from the fire station, we were able to observe from her top floor window the fire fighters exercise by climbing tall ladders and scaling ropes. Other times, they rehearsed playing marches with their tubas and other instruments. On holidays they marched in the center of the city while the children followed them as far as they could, as if following the Pied Piper.

One visit stands out in my memory and still haunts me. I recall standing in the building entrance and hearing a popping sound. People were running in all directions, many falling on top of each other. Horse drawn wagons, piled high with bodies, were being transported somewhere. Mother rushed down, grabbed me in her trembling arms, and ran upstairs to her friend's apartment.

She held me tight and whispered over and over, "Thank you, God, for sparing Irena."

This scene occurred in the area of the Czestochowa Ghetto, where half of the street was still populated by Polish residents and the other was restricted to Jews. What I had witnessed was a daily occurrence, the massacre of Jews being brought by train to Czestochowa.

On Sunday mornings, we usually went for mass at *Jasna Gora*. It was located at the end of the Third Boulevard, approached by a steep walk up the hill. Here one could see a stone wall surrounding the church, and below was a deep depression in the ground covered with trees, bushes, and grass. A statue of Jesus nailed to the cross was located here—"The Way of the Cross." I learned that he carried it to his own crucifixion. We usually came to the unveiling of the Black Madonna icon and stayed through mass until it was covered again. It was always very crowded. On some occasions we saw people crawl on the rough, paved, stone walkway that ended in front of the altar. This was a way they served penance for their sins, hoping for miracles of forgiveness.

I remember an encounter with the evil occupiers. As we walked to *Jasna Gora*, a German soldier smiled at me. I stuck out my tongue at him. He shook his finger disapprovingly. Mother stayed behind me watching in horror. When she caught up with me, she asked, "Irena, why did you do that?"

"Because he killed my daddy," I answered.

In the apartment, across the hallway from us, lived a family of five. The parents kept a low profile during the war because the father, a university professor, was in as much danger as if he had been a Jew. The Nazis were out to destroy the intellectuals so that they would not be a threat to them and so that the Polish masses would be kept in the dark.

To have a radio was a crime. But during the occupation, many people did not surrender their radios and secretly listened for any news in their basements. At the same time, the partisans and underground were distributing leaflets, throwing them from rooftops, telling people to fight the enemy, and that the end of the war was near.

The professor's daughter, Aldona, was a Jew-hater who tried to impose her anti-Semitic beliefs on me. She repeated the stories that were going around that Jews catch little Polish children, kill them, and use their blood for baking matzos for their Jewish holiday Passover. Other children told this story too, and like many of them, I developed a hatred and fear of Jews.

Ghost horror stories were a favorite subject among the adults that lived in our building. The ghost tales kept me up at night and made me afraid to fall asleep. I used to cover my head with the blanket, leaving only a small hole to breathe through. I was afraid that the ghosts' cold hands would reach for me in the darkness of night.

Although Aldona was a few years older, she attached herself to me and became my friend. She was a tall, pretty girl, with long, blonde hair, and a small scar on her upper lip, which intrigued me, but I was afraid to ask how she got it. She wore pretty dresses, which I admired, and wished to have them, too. Her apartment was kept clean with many interesting things that I had never seen before. In particular, there was a jewelry box filled with many colorful embroidery threads. One day when I went to visit Aldona and no one was home, I noticed the open box. I was fascinated by this treasure, wanted it so much, and was tempted to take it. But suddenly I felt uneasy because I remembered that people who steal are punished by being sent to hell. I had learned that hell is a place deep underground where the devil himself is in charge. Hell is where sinners keep burning there for eternity.

Sometimes people dressed up as devils for the holiday *Ostatki*, similar to Halloween in the United States. They wore black bodysuits with a tail swaying. Some also wore devil costumes all in red. The faces were covered with black masks, and horns were affixed to the head. The devils carried large pitchforks in their hands.

Another costume that was very popular was to dress as Orthodox Chasidic Jews. Some wore long dark coats and black hats and glued mustaches, beards, and curled locks of hair as sidelocks to their faces. Also, some glued on long nails and carried black umbrellas. I did not understand the undercurrent as to why the Jewish caricature was used on this holiday.

Mother was most indignant when she saw these people. She never approved or participated in anti-Jewish gossip. She wanted her daughters to be God-fearing people, who would love their neighbors as themselves, just as the Catholic religion championed. She never passed a beggar without giving him some money or bread. My Polish mother taught us to be courteous to strangers, respect elders, be polite to all, and thank people for favors.

My dear mother would stand me next to her and point out how small I was. She promised me that the minute I reached her shoulders, I would be a grownup. Mother always told me what a great helper I was and that I was a good sister to Wilusia by caring for her and carrying her around to protect her. She bragged to her family how good-natured I was. No matter when she would wake me, I would not complain or cry and was always ready to travel on our trading journeys.

4

THE WAR IS ENDING

The city atmosphere changed suddenly in the last days of the German occupation. German soldiers leaving town in a hurry were transporting their possessions and loot in cars and motorcycles. The greed and frenzy extended into our house. Grandpa's biggest obsession was hunting for treasures in homes where the Germans used to live, just as the Germans and their Polish collaborators did to the Jews. Grandpa started to bring in things left by the Nazis that were grabbed from the Jews. He brought a black baby concert piano, a fur coat for Grandma, gold and silver coins, and bronze figurines on marble stands. One figurine fascinated me. It was of a lion with jaws painted bright red to make him look ferocious.

One morning, we heard that the Russian Army was marching toward our town. The people lined the streets greeting the soldiers. They were riding in tanks and vehicles playing lively Russian music on their accordions. People were throwing flowers at the soldiers and embracing them as if the long-awaited liberators were sent by God. I, too, joined the throng of children running after this parade of liberators who smiled at us with friendship.

I was six years old when the war ended. Everyone tried to establish some sort of a normal life. In the summertime, Grandma, Grandpa, Mother, Wilusia, and I used to go to the forest to pick mushrooms and berries. On one of those outings, Aldona joined us. Feeling adventurous, we decided to explore the dense forest on our own. We tried to keep track of our progress, but before long our return path was out of sight. We were hopelessly lost. As evening was approaching, we realized that we needed help and started calling for Mother. She, in the meantime, discovered that we were nowhere in sight and found a forest ranger to help look for us. Finally, late that night, frightened, hungry, cold, and crying, we were reunited with our families.

My other childhood friends were Tozik and his sister Ala. They too, like Grandpa and Grandma Maj, were refugees from the Russian Revolution. According to Grandma Jozefa, they came with their widowed mother and five siblings. Their situation was worse than ours. Grandma used to send them food because even after the war they had nothing.

I admired and was intrigued by Tozik and Ala's mother. She had an aristocratic air about her. Her beauty was still evident, even after the hardships of the war. She had the typical high cheekbones of the Slavic beauties. Often, she wore her plush red velvet robe and large gold hoop earrings as if to bring back an aura of her previous aristocratic life. Her black hair was streaked with gray and braided, intertwined with ribbons, which she wore wrapped around her head like a crown. This braid style evoked something in my memory, but I didn't know why. Eventually this image clarified this memory.

The girls and Tozik inherited their mother's distinguished good looks. Mrs. Drozdow never bothered with housework; it was beneath her upper-class upbringing. She often spoke about her attending the same girls' school as the Czar's daughters.

As I grew older and attained some understanding of survival skills, I stunned both Grandpa and myself by changing his behavior towards me. My daily chore was to help him pull off and shine his boots, even when he was drunk. If I didn't do it fast enough and to his liking, he cursed and pointed to the rabbit's foot strap that hung in the living room for everyone to see. These threats were fearsome and humiliated me. They diminished my confidence. Somehow, I gathered strength to finally speak up for myself.

This resolve happened when I observed that when Grandpa fell asleep in his drunken stupor, a horsefly flew into his mouth, which caused him to choke and cough. Then, without knowing, he swallowed the unwelcome stray insect. So, I came to the conclusion that he was vulnerable in his sleep. That morning I told him that if he didn't stop hitting me, I would tie him. As soon as these words came out of my mouth, I trembled in fear and amazement that I dared such a threat. As I looked apprehensively at his face, I discovered that this time he had a scared look. Maybe he was sober for the first time, because after this event, he stopped spanking me.

Mother and Grandma also developed a strategy to prevent Grandpa's violence. When we saw him through the window swaggering drunk into the front yard, I was instructed to offer him more vodka. This helped keep him drunk, and although he still created a lot of damage in the house, he had no energy to continue a long rampage, and collapsed into a torpor almost immediately. Nevertheless, Grandma remained his favorite victim, upon whom he dished out violence until the day he died. I made a promise that when I grew up and became a mother, I would never humiliate or spank my children.

Jasna Gora attracted more and more people who were coming to thank God for the end of the war, or maybe they expected miracles to put their lives together. It was called *pielgrzymki* (pilgrimage). The sick and handicapped with crutches were looking for miraculous healing for which the church was famous.

On Sundays, merchants set up their tables full of religious relic souvenirs, wooden toys made by local artisans, cotton candy, and colorful rock candy sold in chunks. There were ice cream and lemonade stands to tempt and refresh.

Church of St. Zigmunt © by sheris9/ shutterstock.com

Ida, Grandfather Maj and Wilusia with ice cream, circa 1946.

Across from *Jasna Gora,* at the other end of the First Boulevard, was the Church of St. Zigmunt where I was christened, and where I attended Easter services.

At Easter time, Mother, like others in our town, prepared a wicker basket lined with a hand-made doily and filled with painted and colored eggs that I learned to hand paint. We used natural colors—brown from boiled onion-skins, green from spinach, and red from beets. The most interesting and best tasting treats were lambs and bunnies made of sugar which were painted in pretty colors and decorated with gold.

On Easter Sunday, we waited in a long line, carrying these baskets and treats, for the priest to bless with holy water. The exhilaration of the occasion, the statues of saints, richly decorated altars, walls adorned with angels, beautiful organ music playing in the background, and the sweet scent of the burning leaves made me feel that this was what heaven must be like.

Our first Easter after the war, was even more meaningful when Grandpa and Grandma were informed that her family, who had just arrived from Russia, was at the train station waiting to be picked up. The newcomers were Minia, Grandma Jozefa's sister, her daughter, Hala, and son, Feliks. I scrutinized them with curiosity. I was in awe that my family became bigger. We had more people.

5

A PAINFUL TRANSITION — WHO AM I?

When the war ended, the Jews who returned to Czestochowa organized an agency to assist surviving families in finding each other and help supply housing and jobs. They even started an orphanage for children with Hebrew studies which prepared them to immigrate to Palestine. I was six years old, but physically I looked like three. Hunger and lice gave me that distinct, gaunt, big-eyed look of a child who witnessed too much for her age.

Life was very hard for Mother, as she tried to keep our family fed and sheltered. And since we still shared the small apartment with Grandma and Grandpa, out of desperation to get away from her abusive father-in-law, she decided to appeal to the Jewish Agency for help, admitting that she saved a Jewish child during the German occupation. She was quickly relocated to a new apartment, only half a block from Grandpa, on the corner of Katedralna and Swierczewskiego Streets. The Jewish Committee gave her this apartment with the understanding that she would allow me to attend Hebrew studies in a house of worship.

When Mother left me at the synagogue in the morning, anxiety of being in a strange place, with strange people, who spoke a language I did not understand, brought me to hysterical tears. The prayers were not what I heard at home or in church. The bearded men, wrapped in white shawls trimmed with black stripes and tassels, and wearing hats or round black skull caps, terrified me. I quickly came to the conclusion that I was among the terrible "blood-thirsty" Jews

33

that the crowd of children constantly talked about. I was sure that these were the Jews that would kill me and use my blood for matzos for their Passover holiday. My panic grew, and I decided that at the first opportunity I must run away from them.

The Jewish Committee, seeing my inability to adjust, came to the conclusion that the safest place for me and in general for Jews who survived, was in Palestine. And so, this plan was being brought to realization by having one of the committee members volunteer to take me to the railroad station with a *dorozka* (horse- drawn carriage) and then to Palestine.

Sensing that I was being taken away, I started to scream, "Help, help, good people! The Jews have kidnapped me to use my blood for matzo!"

It took only a few seconds for a crowd to gather around us. Even police showed up and asked the woman to identify herself. The moment she let go of my hand, I ran as fast as I could to Grandfather's apartment, rather than to Mother Jozefa, because I felt she had betrayed me. I told Grandpa what happened and that I did not want to return to Mother. I never returned to live with her again.

The Jewish Committee tried to convince Grandfather that I belonged to them, but he flatly refused and even threatened to kill anyone with an ax who came to his doorstep asking for me. Until this time, he believed that I was his son's natural daughter. When he learned the truth about me, he became greedy and told the Committee that he was the one who stuck his neck out for me during the war. No credit was given to my mother, Jozefa. Grandpa Maj started bragging to neighbors and friends that he was preparing, sewing for himself a large pocket for the money the Jews would pay him for my return.

My successful escape was big news in Poland in the Jewish circles. The Jewish community was troubled about what might happen if a crowd got angry at Jews. Even at this time, evil, anti-Semitic hate mongers murdered many after the war, such as the pogrom in Kielce.

Only three of my mother's sisters survived. Aunt Zosia, Mother's youngest sister was hidden by a Polish man whom she married. They had twins, a boy and a girl, but only the boy survived. He was named Bogdan.

Aunt Sonia returned to Sosnowiec to rejoin the surviving family. She survived most of the war with the partisans in the forests of Poland. Her daughter Gienia died of pneumonia only a few weeks before liberation.

My Aunt Roma, who survived with her husband Joe in Siberia, came back to live in Sosnowiec. She questioned with hope when she heard the news about this willful child.

"This may be our Ida who was given by my sister Rozia to a man in Czestochowa," she exclaimed. "We must go to check it out. Such a smart child. She must be ours."

My Aunt Roma and Uncle Joe went to his sister Lena in Czestochowa and learned from the Jewish Committee where the little troublemaker lived. They stood across the street from our building for hours, watching me play in the front yard. I was about the age of my sister, Gienia, when they had seen her last. They were stunned by the resemblance and all agreed that by the grace of God, I survived the war.

In 1946, my father returned from Russia to Sosnowiec. As a Polish soldier, the German's took him prisoner, and somehow the Polish soldiers were recaptured by the Russian Army and sent to work in the mines of the southern part of the Soviet Union.

When Father learned about the tragedy of my mother's suicide and losing the children, a glimmer of hope was relayed to him that Ida, one of the twins, may have survived. The family advised Father to take a train to Czestochowa and get in touch with the local Jewish Committee. He produced all the facts known to him and asked for their advice on how to get his daughter back, if it was indeed his daughter.

Dr. Goldberg was a well-known figure and personality in the Jewish community. After reviewing all the facts with Father and looking at the few family pictures Father presented, he said, "My dear Mr. Paluch, I'm almost positive that we know where your daughter is. She is the little troublemaker who almost started a pogrom in our city. She resides with an old drunkard Grandfather who does not open his door to anyone unless he smells a big profit for himself."

Nonetheless, Father and the doctor walked to Street Katerdralna 14 to see me. They found me playing outside in the front yard, and just as my aunts and Uncle Joe recognized me, Father did too.

He turned to Dr. Goldberg and said, "The similarities are incredible. She even skips on the edge of the sidewalk like Gienia used to."

My father started to cry, but Dr. Goldberg advised him to save his tears and talk to Mr. Maj immediately. They knocked on the first door on the right, which Grandpa opened. Dr. Goldberg introduced the newcomer as Irena's father. Grandpa did not exhibit his usual hot temper and instead invited them in. He made sure that Father understood his role in saving my life during the war. There was not even a mention of Jozefa. He finally presented his outrageous demand.

"I stuck my neck out for her," he told Father.

"She was like my own granddaughter. I loved her and fed her and took care of her at a great risk to me and the rest of my family."

He continued, "I deserve a reward. You people are very rich, and I want you to give me a million *zloty* for my sacrifices during the war."

Father sat stunned in disbelief. He tried to reason with Grandpa but to no avail. He pleaded with him saying that he had just arrived from Russia with one shirt on his back. He implored Grandpa, saying that he was still shaken after learning about his wife's and two children's tragic deaths.

Finally, Father told Grandpa, "I don't know if it is within human power to reward you for what you have done. Only God himself can repay you for your brave heart. I can only go to my family and raise some money but not the amount you are demanding from me."

When they parted, Father got a promise from Grandfather that he would be allowed to visit me so we could become acquainted until the money was delivered, and I would be surrendered to Father.

At first Father went to the local courthouse to present his case. He even left the photographs he had of us. But the case was never resolved, so the only alternative was to look for ransom money.

On his first visit, Father was introduced to me as Uncle Leon. At the suggestion of Dr. Goldberg, Father wore a visible cross in order to remove any suspicions that he was a Jew. He brought candy and played with me for hours. I made him carry me around on his shoulders so I could kiss all the icons of the saints hanging on the walls. I was too young to understand what pain I was causing him by my behavior. Yet, he was grateful that his child was alive.

On one of his visits, Father took out two pictures out of his wallet. He showed me the first one, which was a picture of a woman.

He asked me, "Irena, do you know this lady?" My immediate answer was, "This is my mother."

The distant memory of her image was still with me. I had dreams about her and about my twin brother and sister, Genia, but they were vague and fleeting. Of course, I was too young to understand what it meant or to question it. Then he showed me the other picture, which I also recognized. I remembered Mother showing it to us and saying, "This man in the middle is your father." But the man standing in front of me now did not look like the one in the picture. This man was old, with a tired skinny face and some gray hair. He looked like a hopeless soul.

In time, Father managed to gather money through the Jewish self- help organizations, plus the contributions from my mother's

Father Chaim/Leon and Ida, 1947.

sisters, Roma, Zosia, and Sonia. They shared with Father the profit from selling my maternal grandfather's home in Szczekociny.

In the meantime, Mother Jozefa pleaded and begged for Grandfather Maj not to go through with his money-grubbing scheme. But to no avail, his concern and focus was the money that would be delivered to him. Mother Jozefa never benefited from the money that was paid for me. Grandpa kept it all and spent every last *grosz* (cent) getting drunk.

Careful arrangements were made to take me back to Sosnowiec. On the day that Father was scheduled to arrive, Aldona, who had learned about my being returned to Father, conducted her own rescue mission. She hid me in the dark, slimy basement of our building to save me from being kidnapped by the Jews. I was grateful to Aldona for hiding me because I was petrified of what would happen to me at the hands of the Jews if I were taken away.

I was cowering in my hiding place, fearful that I would be heard as my bony body trembled uncontrollably. The rats and mice were scampering around me, and any contact with the slimy, damp walls threw me into panic and repulsion of touching the many snails that crept up and down. Everybody was searching frantically for me, everyone except Jozefa, who was not told that I was leaving. Finally, Aldona's parents forced her to bring me out of the basement, and to my relief, escaping the disgusting hiding place.

I was shoved into a taxicab kicking and screaming and was forced to sit on my father's lap. He restrained my hands as I swore and shouted, "Let me go!" adding, "Too bad Hitler didn't finish you Jews off!"

I struggled like a tiger fighting for my life, but somehow Father was able to hold on to me. When we arrived at Aunt Lyla's apartment in Sosnowiec, I was hysterical and out of control. I wanted to get to the window and jump. All I could think of was that I was again in the hands of Jews.

The more Father tried to calm me, the more violent I became. I scratched his and my face until we both were bleeding. I cried and sobbed until exhaustion and sleep overtook me. When I woke up the next morning and looked around, I was in a beautiful child's bed with silk and lace covers that my aunt readied for me. I discovered that my chain with a medallion of Jesus had disappeared from my neck. I became frightened that now there was no God to protect me. At this immature age, I had to deal with such fearful questions and choices. My mind was in turmoil and burdened with plans of how to escape from this Jew who held me against my will.

Because the only clothing I had was what I was wearing, Aunt Lyla advised Father to go to town to visit the Jewish charitable organizations. The clerk at the office led us to large rooms where all kinds of clothing and shoes were displayed. I was given free rein to choose, which was not a wise decision on Father's part, but it made him appear kind to me. Everything that was colorful ended up in our bag. Immediately I took off my dirty clothes and put on a fresh white blouse and a red pleated skirt.

The office clerk fixed my hair with a large ribbon and suggested that Father have a picture taken as I looked that day. We went to a photo studio where the photographer posed me in an appealing way. The picture must have made quite an impression on the photographer because he displayed it in the window of his studio for many years. That picture later changed my life.

The picture that changed my life, circa 1946.

6

LIFE IN A JEWISH CHILDREN'S HOME

Since Father was a widower and did not have a place of his own, he decided to temporarily put me in a Jewish children's home in the city of Zabrze, not far from Sosnowiec. He took me on the tram that ran between the two cities.

We arrived at a guarded entrance gate of a red brick building. The staff, who cared for about eighty Jewish children who survived the Holocaust, welcomed us. The children were retrieved from Polish families who hid them and saved their lives. Most of them were orphans. Some were returned by courageous Polish people who understood that their role as protector was over when the war ended.

Other children were discovered by Captain Druker who helped organize orphanages all over Poland. The Captain was most helpful to Father in obtaining funds that ultimately went to Grandpa Maj. Captain Druker was a beloved and respected man in the Jewish children's homes.

The children at the Zabrze orphanage called Yeshayahu Drucker "*Pan Kapitan*," Sir Captain. The children attached themselves to him like to a father. The children at Zabrze were very needy. He made sure that each child received individual attention, which they had been deprived of for the war years, as they had been orphaned. He maintained contact with the children until they left Poland and even later continued the communications when they were all in Israel. To him these children were part of the surviving nation that had to be nurtured and restored to life.

I finally began to feel comfortable at the orphanage and was happy
to get rid of Father, the Jew. At this stage, I did not suspect that the
children were Jewish. They all spoke Polish. The older children were
helping the younger ones, and the staff did everything possible to
make the children happy.

We were kept clean and were offered lots of good food. Most had
no appetite and were suffering a longing for the families that hid
them. It was a very strange group of lost little souls. Some tried to run
away, but they were usually found and brought back after a few hours
of adventure that made them hungry and scared. One of the girls
kept a red scar on her neck hidden. The rumor was that the birth
parents made the mark when she was an infant, before they gave her
away, so they would be able to recognize her after the war.

During the day, we were sent to a local public school together
with the Polish children. It was to give us a more normal setting and
keep us distracted to think less of running away. After school, the
activities were structured around culture, learning to play piano, and
a serious study of the Jewish religion. I learned my new prayers and
the blessings before a meal, and when entering a doorway, I kissed
the *mezuzah,* (Jewish religious object) which was hung on the door
frame.

Slowly, I adjusted and grew to like the people around me. Soon it
didn't bother me that they were Jewish. Any free time and evenings
were devoted to playing with friends. This also kept me busy and
distracted my immature mind from brooding about my lost Polish
family—missing Mother Jozefa. But many times, a longing for them
returned.

Of course, as with most groups of children, the games sometimes
turned cruel. I remember an instance when a new girl was given
something foul to drink by an established clique of girls. This episode
made the staff very angry, and we were more closely supervised after
that event.

As the Jewish holidays were approaching, we were taught about
the coming holiday of *Sukkot.* This was a holiday celebrating the forty

years of wandering in the desert, after the Exodus from Egypt, and thanking God for the harvest. The children were involved in building and decorating the *sukkah* in the front yard, which was built of trellised walls and a roof. Eating treats in this airy structure was new and fun.

On *Simchas Torah*, the holiday of receiving the Ten Commandments, we were given apples on sticks and little blue and white flags to carry to the *sukkah*. The spirit, music, and cheerfulness of the season began to look and feel joyous. I started to accept more and more that these Jews in the orphanage weren't so bad. They did not scare me anymore. They were acting the same as the children and adults I knew in Czestochowa. I was beginning to know Jews as they really were, not as the non-Jewish neighbors and children had portrayed them to me.

7

LIFE WITH MY STEPMOTHER IN WROCLAW

As soon as I started to feel that I belonged, under the protection of the Jewish children's home, Father showed up and took me back to the city of Wroclaw. He chose that city, in part, because he did not think Jozefa could find me there.

Father had married Cyvia Knopf, an Aushwitz survivor. She was a squat woman with heavy hips and big bosoms. She had cold, blue eyes, a sharp, long nose, and thin lips that rarely formed a smile. She did not exude welcome nor warmth toward me. When she did smile, it was a strange grimace, a mask that hid all feelings.

I always wondered what Father saw in this unattractive woman. Most likely, he didn't think about it too much when he married her. Right after the war, people married just about anyone, just to have a family, just to have someone to be with and not be alone. Many of these marriages would not have occurred before the war. As the proverb says, "War makes strange bedfellows." I think perhaps Father may have been impressed that Cyvia was from a *Chasidic* (orthodox rabbinic family) and although he was of a more modern persuasion, he may have been captivated that she represented the aristocratic connections by Jewish standards.

We lived in an apartment on the third floor on Olbinska Street, which we shared with another couple, Mr. and Mrs. Szwarc. We shared a large kitchen with bedrooms on either side for each family. Mr. Szwarc was a tailor like Father.

One evening, I was sitting at the table where Father was cutting fabrics. Cyvia was also sitting at the table. She and I were arguing about something. Not able to tolerate this abuse, I jumped from the table to get away from the scene. Father misunderstood my reaction and thought that I was jumping angrily at Cyvia. He grabbed the ruler and slapped my bottom.

I reacted to this reprimand by crying hysterically. Consciously or maybe to let out my unhappiness from Cyvia's maltreatment and to punish Father when I saw that he was in shock, I sobbed louder and complained that my back hurt. I went to bed and continued to cry. After a time, Father came to my room and apologized—he could not stand my crying. I accused him of being just like Grandpa Maj. After this event, he never touched me again. But the sermons he gave me every day before I left for school were worse than spankings.

Mr. and Mrs. Szwarc were affectionate towards me and always offered me something to eat. On many occasions. Mrs. Szwarc invited me to come with her for food shopping. In contrast to them, my stepmother was a bitter, sarcastic, unpleasant woman who resented me from the start. She used to bemoan her luck and questioned out loud why I had survived while her dear boys had been gassed in Aushwitz. I was too young to understand why she was taking her loss out on me. When Cyvia had a headache, she lay in bed with a cold compress on her forehead and was vicious toward me. She hid food from me, and our house was always dirty and in disarray.

As I matured, I understood the twisted mind of Cyvia, who lost faith in God and, full of resentment, blamed her tragedy on everyone that survived. Cyvia suffered flashbacks of her experiences in the death camps, which she survived in the most harsh ways.

Once I overheard her confide to Father about striking her sister-in- law on the head over a scrap of bread, which caused the woman to die from the injury. The family never forgave her. This information put the fear of God in my heart for the rest of my life knowing that her violence had caused someone's death.

One day in 1947, coming home from school, Mrs. Szwarc informed me that Father and Cyvia moved across the street. I was shocked by this news, especially since no one even bothered to tell me. I was not prepared for this move. Even at this young age, I questioned my place in this family and my father's commitment to me.

The apartment, No. 4, on the second floor at Olbinska 12, consisted of two-bedrooms with a balcony, which was my only delight. The entrance and stairway were damp, dark, and scary and always smelled of urine. Mice and rats were everywhere, although, by this point in my short life, I was accustomed to sharing space with these creatures.

Father registered me at the newly-organized Sholom Aleichem Jewish school. The school was at the edge of town, between mountains of rubble of war-torn buildings. It was named after a famous Jewish writer, whose portrayal of the severe life and persecution of Jews in little towns and villages throughout Poland and Russia became classics. He was equated as the Jewish Mark Twain.

Fields of bricks surrounded the whole area of Wroclaw. The unexploded bombs and grenades were a daily danger to all. They claimed many victims, especially children who played in the rubble.

In many areas, people lived in half-demolished buildings, without heat or electricity. Because Father was ingenious and quick thinking, we had gas light in our kitchen. This came about when Father saw gas street lamps being installed in front of our building. He bribed the installer to connect gas lights to the already existing gas pipes in our ceiling. Since electricity was not available, we at least had some dim light. Father worked late into the night sewing on the Singer machine driven by a foot pedal.

When Father brought me to school, I was seven years old, but because I was very small and frail and looked much younger, he could not convince the teachers to place me in the first grade without a birth certificate. So, I was put in kindergarten with a very scary teacher,

Mrs. Maria. She was tall and weighed over two hundred pounds. Her elephant- like legs could hardly carry the bulk of her body. It amazed me that in this war that starved thousands, she could be this heavy. She always wore a black silk dress and combed her silver-gray hair in a bun. Mrs. Maria was not the perfect teacher, but she had her own way of keeping the youngsters in line.

On too many occasions, she punished the unruly child by placing the little one on her lap, slipping down the underwear, and spanking the naked bottom until it was red. She then put the crying and embarrassed child in the corner of the room for an hour or so, and then the child was allowed to go back to the daily activities.

We were involved in many activities. We acted out fairytale stories that Mrs. Maria read to us. We performed a play for the parents, under her direction. The first play was Snow White and the Seven Dwarfs. The role of Snow White came down to a choice between me and the school director's daughter, Dita, who got the part. But during our recess playtime, the classmates chose me to be Snow White when we acted out the story.

Our school was a three-story red brick building surrounded by a front and back yard. It had been a school before the war, but at the end of war, German soldiers were housed there, as evidenced by the dark green, heavy canvas cots that were stored in the basement. A white tiled kitchen, with large pots, was used as our cafeteria. The school had a lab room and a large gym, which was well-equipped, compared to most other schools. Children who lived far away, like me, were able to sleep over at the school on cold winter nights.

8

JEWISH HOLIDAYS

In the spring of 1947, Passover was the one time of the year when Cyvia cleaned the apartment and made me do the dirtiest chores. I rubbed and scrubbed the wooden floor on my hands and knees. After it dried, I applied a red-paste wax and waited for the wax to dry. Again, on hands and knees, I polished it with an old woolen rag. Cyvia covered the floors with newspapers until the first day of Passover.

She also had a ritual of taking a bath once a week in the aluminum tub. The water was heated in large pots on top of the stove and tempered with cold water. She was the first in the tub, followed by Father, and I was last. By that time, the water was cold and dirty.

Each morning it was my duty to start the oven. One of my chores was to carry up a load of damp wood and coal from the basement. It took many tries to get the fire going. Cyvia would not roll out of bed until the rooms were warm.

The soot and ashes had to be cleaned out every day. The ashes that fell through the grill at the bottom of the oven were not wasted. They were used to scrub the pots and pans, and during winter, they were scattered on the slippery sidewalks in front of our building. It was a harsh and hard task for a frail child—I felt like Cinderella.

The cold winter displayed a wonderland show on our windowpanes. The indescribable frost designs affected my imagination to visualize our rooms as Cinderella's magic ice castle. The rooms were so cold that one could see one's breath.

Passover was a sign that spring and warmer weather was on the way. I hoped for an end to my hard chores. In preparation for the holiday, Cyvia started koshering all our dishes. She soaked them in a tub of boiling, hot water and suspended each on a string to dry in the sun on our balcony. To make the Passover koshering process easier, she did not bring in milk products into the house and thus would not have a problem of keeping meat and milk dishes separated.

The holiday preparations brought forth untapped energies for my usually unenergetic stepmother. Days in advance she bought a live carp fish, which became my pet. She put it in our aluminum tub but only until the day when she started cooking for the holiday. On that day, she proceeded to hit the fish's head with a hammer in order to kill it. The first blows did not do the job. The poor fish wriggled and stubbornly hung to life. But Cyvia was determined and, of course, succeeded.

Her plates of chicken soup included floating feathers. Cyvia's method of cooking always made one wary what one was eating. It was fatty, burned, too salty, spoiled, and often made us sick. Her determination to succeed was evident when she bought a goose and force-fed it *kluski,* (dumplings). They were made from flour and water, which she stuffed down the poor goose's throat with her index finger. When Cyvia had no goose, she kept a chicken in a cage on our balcony.

One day, when she was checking the chicken's posterior for fat accumulation, the chicken slipped out of her hands and flew off the balcony and ran down the street. Cyvia ran after the fowl asking me to help catch it. I joined in the chase, but the scared bird succeeded in keeping ahead of us, continuing down the block. It flew into the open doors of the church and disappeared inside. Cyvia ran after it screaming for help. Luckily, there was no one inside but the priest. He too started to run after the chicken, trying to prevent it from damaging the church. The chicken was eventually caught, and Cyvia got a warning from the priest not to keep animals on the balcony.

She came home exhausted, decided not to tell Father about this embarrassing incident, and made me swear not to tell. The ongoing jokes and teasing by the neighborhood children were that the chicken wanted to convert to Catholicism. As I recall my distressed young years, I cannot forget the comedy that was played out on occasions.

9

FIRST GRADE

The summer of 1947, when I was about seven years old, I was sent with the rest of the children to summer camp in Wiselka. We stayed in a large building by the beach, where we spent most of the time splashing in the Baltic Sea. Food was still scarce. Only bread and eggs were plentiful. Parents sent food packages, and some came to help out with the cooking and guard the facilities. I was one of the few that did not get packages, but in every letter, Father sent me some money, so I was able to buy some snacks. I bought candy and little brooches made of seashells that were hand painted by local people.

In the afternoons, we spent time at the beach, looking for shells and amber that the water washed ashore. On cold days, we sat lined up on the beach in enclosed, large, padded, wicker armchairs. We were covered with blankets and told to lie still and absorb as much sun and fresh sea air as possible. We were impatient to move and play, but the cold forced us to lie there as mummies.

On one of the sunny days, a photographer came to the beach, and I had him take a smiling picture of me in a borrowed sailor's hat. The other children liked this idea of wearing a sailor's hat, so all followed my example. It seemed that I had set a trend because many people on the beach had their picture taken in sailor hats. The photographer had an unexpected windfall. I was sad to see the carefree, happy summer days end, but I was looking forward to returning to school and this time, to first grade.

On the first morning, all were gathered in the small assembly hall. Words of advice were given to the first graders, "Be polite to the teachers, neighbors, and schoolmates. Greet each other in the morning, show respect to older people on the trams and offer them your seat."

The thirty-some students were assigned to two rooms, "A" and "B," which caused a lot of rivalry between us. We all wanted to earn good grades and represent our school with honor. The teachers were dedicated and treated us with special care. The sentiment in those days was that every Jewish child that survived was precious. We felt as if our schoolmates and teachers were our extended family. In years to follow, we grew attached to each other for the rest of our lives.

Each morning, we were lined up in the corridor and given a gagging potion of cod liver oil that was doled out to each child with the same unwashed spoon. It was supposed to improve our appetite, helping us to gain weight. Many were repulsed by the taste and wound up vomiting the reputed curative elixir. In addition, everyone had to go through a cleanliness check performed by a teacher. He or she checked our ears to see if they were clean to make sure "potatoes were not growing inside." They also checked the length of our nails, which had to be clean and cut short. But most importantly, the white collar of our school uniform had to be clean. If anything was not right, we were sent home with a note to our parents. This inspection, conducted in front of all the students, was a great embarrassment and deflated one's self-esteem and confidence.

I was very short for my age, and since my last name was Paluch, which translates to "thumb" in Polish, the children gave me a nickname, *Tomcio Paluszek*, which is derived from the famous children's story, Tom Thumb—the tiny boy who was small as a thumb. As much as the nickname bothered me, I never expected that it would be an important identifying clue, a key to my endless, life-long search.

To help rebuild Wroclaw from the ruins, many workers and school children volunteered to sort old undamaged bricks from the mountains of demolished buildings, and stacked them neatly in rows. Trucks picked up the salvaged bricks, which were then reused to build new buildings. We did not mind doing this work because we were enthusiastic to contribute in rebuilding a new future for our Polish homeland.

Another activity that our school participated in was helping pick the corn crops on the commune farms. On Sundays, we were transported in military trucks to help pick these crops. Being city kids, we knew very little about agriculture and most probably did more damage to the fields than help. Most of the time we were hungry and hid some of the corn in our clothes to take

Ida, 1947.

home. Our return ride home was spent singing and showing off who had more calluses on their hands.

The following summer, I went to summer camp by the Baltic Sea, but this time we were in a place called *Darlowko*. The beach was a gathering place for many other summer campers from all over Poland. In the early morning, we marched to the beach lined up in double rows, flying a white and red Polish flag and returned at lunchtime to our run-down building where we stayed.

That summer left me with a lifelong fear of deep water. Most of the children, including me, didn't know how to swim. We enjoyed holding on to the rocky water breakers as the incoming waves showered us with their power. Unexpectedly, I stepped into a drop-off and found myself under water gulping for air, choking on the salty water. My exhilaration and carefree sea experience suddenly became a nightmare. I panicked, not knowing how to save myself. Suddenly, I felt a wave pick me up and carry me to higher ground. It felt almost miraculous that caring arms lifted me out of this danger.

That day I promised to never go into deep water and never again to vacation by the sea. I shared this experience with other children who also experienced similar frights of almost drowning. This place served as a symbol of a struggle to save myself.

10

GRANDPA MAJ COMES LOOKING FOR ME

My life with Father and Cyvia became routine, but occasionally the longing for Mother Jozefa and Wilusia would crop up. Often, I wondered how they were and if they were missing me as much as I missed them.

One day a classmate came running to tell me that a strange man was claiming to be my grandfather, and that he had a picture to prove it. When I heard this, I got very anxious and thought it must be Grandpa Maj, the devil himself. Hesitatingly, I went to the entrance, and sure enough, it was.

In great distress and panic, I ran to the teachers' conference room, crying hysterically and spilling out my painful wartime suffering at the hands of this man. My teacher immediately went to speak to Grandpa Maj who reassured the teacher that he meant no harm. His family missed me desperately, and he was accused by his friends and neighbors of selling a Polish child to the Jews. He explained that the only thing he wanted was to prove them wrong, that he did the honorable thing by giving a daughter back to her real father.

The teacher decided to take me home in a cab and sent Grandpa Maj in another to meet with my father. When Father heard about the situation, he came out with my stepmother to talk to Grandpa. He was crying and begging Father to let me come to Czestochowa for a visit. He also promised that he would stop drinking. Somehow Father came to an agreement, and it was decided that in a few weeks my stepmother, Cyvia, would take me to Czestochowa to visit them.

Wilusia Maj and Ida, 1950.

I was very eager to see Mother Jozefa, Wilusia, and Grandma Jozefa. When we finally arrived in Czestochowa, we were greeted with a feast, including a baked ham. In the past, Grandma was not much of a hostess. For this occasion, she overcame her usual distaste for entertaining. Of course, Cyvia refused to eat the ham, and instead we ate the matzo and oranges we brought for our hosts. As soon as I had a chance, I left Cyvia to stay with Grandma to complain about me. I only had one purpose and that was to run straight to Mother Jozefa. She greeted me at her door with open arms, embracing me with tenderness that melts my heart to this day. She looked at me with disbelief at how I had grown and matured. We had not seen each other for three years. Wilusia, my Polish sister, greeted me with a warm, loving gladness too.

Mother looking at the two of us said with tears flowing, "Here are my daughters together again."

On Sunday, we all had a picnic in the woods, commemorated with a picture of the event of our reunion. After this successful visit, from then on, Father allowed me to spend some summers and Christmas vacations with the Maj family.

Wilusia gave me her caged pet rabbit as a going away gift. The rabbit was placed on our balcony. Every day, I went out to gather grass and bought carrots for my new pet. One day, when I returned from school, dinner was ready, which was a rare occurrence in our home. Cyvia was in an unusually good humor. She urged me to eat quickly and go to play outdoors. When I was ready to leave, she asked me if I enjoyed the dinner. I answered yes. Then, with her strange grimaced smile, she said, "It was your rabbit!"

I felt such rage and hatred towards Cyvia, and I promised revenge. I drew a caricature of her as a witch flying on a broom, and underneath I wrote, "Here lives the biggest witch of them all on 12 Olbinska Street." I placed it in our mailbox. Obviously, she found the note and showed it to Father. A huge fight followed, and I insisted that Father let me return to Jozefa or let me live in the Jewish Children's Home that had moved from the neighboring town of Dzierzoniow.

Most of the resident children attended our school and seemed happy, well-dressed, and had wonderful friendships. I really envied them because they did not have to suffer a real-life stepmother as Sholom Aleichem had written about in his classic books. I felt close to him and could identify with the suffering he endured from his stepmother.

I pleaded with Father, who really knew the truth but had no courage to speak up. His only response to me was, "And what will the people say? How will I look in their eyes?" So, we continued this unhappy, stress-filled relationship for many more years.

11

COMING OF AGE

By the third grade, I was classified by our homeroom teacher, Mr. Brandes, as a leader of the "aristocrats"—the elite of our class. Lusia Wajntraub, my lifelong friend, was accepted to our clique when she came to our school after all the Hebrew schools were closed. Our school was the only Jewish school in town.

In the early years after the war, there were some Zionist organizations in Wroclaw. They attracted the young to their gatherings, where dancing and singing Hebrew songs lifted our spirits and awakened a yearning for Israel, a country of our own. But as quickly as these organizations appeared, so they disappeared.

Some of the children emigrated to Israel with their parents, including the twins Hana and Fella, who were my good friends. I was drawn to them with an unusual curiosity and could not specifically identify this mysterious longing. Mother Jozefa did tell me that I had siblings, especially a twin, but I could not connect that they were real. My memories were fractured and absorbed by the present life. When Lusia shared a secret that her parents applied to immigrate to Israel, I mentioned it to Father. He told me in confidence that he had applied every year but we were always refused.

On most Sundays, I visited with a girlfriend Renia. We played with rag dolls that we made in school or with our own homemade paper cutout dolls and paper clothes. As we became teenagers, our interest focused outside the building, across the street where boys waved and called us. The transition from dolls to an interest in boys inspired us to seek out the boys from the higher grades. We wanted to grow up fast.

When Father wasn't around, I taught myself to use his sewing machine. He usually knew when I used it because I always managed to break the needle. When he was at work, I decided to sew a black corduroy skirt and tight blouse with a low-cut neckline, just like Gina Lollobrigida wore in one of her movies. When I finished these items, I proudly paraded in the street and got some curious looks from people. I interpreted the stares to mean I was attractive and exceptionally grownup. When Father came home, and the neighbors told him that his fourteen-year-old daughter strutted around in a sexy getup, he gave me a long lecture about how a lady must look and present herself. I was firmly told to wear a turtleneck under the sexy shirt.

Besides being interested in fashion, Renia and I were intrigued by and admired American rock and roll music. Attending some college dances, we were exposed to the music of Elvis Presley, whose records had infiltrated even the Iron Curtain. We wanted to look and act like the young people in the Western World that we saw in the movies. But for now, all we could do was carry our backpacks under our arms instead on our backs so they would look like purses. We molded the beret, that was part of our school uniform, into another shape, and the uniform was replaced by street clothes, which we kept in our backpacks until needed.

We were planning our future together. We dreamed and planned that after high school, we would attend Warsaw University and live in the same dorm. And a better dream would be if our entire class would live there too until we earned our degrees.

Life was a struggle. The *Zelazna Kurtyna* (Iron Curtain) was a political divide that was established by both the East and West, (America in the West, and the Soviet Union in the East). Shortages of basic needs lasted from the time of WWII until "Solidarity" won independence from the Communists.

12

MY AUNTS LEAVE POLAND

My three aunts left Poland in 1946 and went to the American Zone in Berlin. From there, Aunt Roma and Uncle Joe settled in Chicago in 1948. Aunt Sonia married a Holocaust survivor she met at the displaced person's camp in Germany, and they too immigrated to Chicago. They eventually moved to Sao Paulo, Brazil.

The entry into my teenage years was embellished with beautiful things that Aunt Sonia sent me from Brazil. Many packages arrived from all her travels, which surprised and delighted me. These packages were not only a treasure, but also a glimpse of what the world was like outside drab Poland. She sent me colored pencils in a beautiful box, adorned with a picture of the snow-covered Matterhorn Mountain. When I opened the box, to my great pleasure, I found a row of some thirty-two rainbow- colored pencils and a sharpener, which was an unattainable object in Poland. Prior to the arrival of this precise little sharpening tool, we used to sharpen pencils with a kitchen knife, or at best, with an old, used razor blade. Each package made me *ooh* and *ahh* with delight, in disbelief that such things existed in this world.

Aunt Sonia also surprised me with packages of beautiful clothing, which made me feel guilty and embarrassed to wear them outside the house. When I did walk outside in my imported elegant, colorful, and of course, unusual outfits, I felt like the best dressed child in Poland. It caused people to stare at me.

13

PROPAGANDA

As students got older, more classrooms and subjects were presented to accommodate the Communist dogma. Very soon a high school level was added to our school. More teachers joined the staff, although not all were Jewish. The authority of the Communist administration influenced and affected the subjects and study materials. Pressure to join the Communist Party came not only from the teachers but also from students.

At this time, our living quarters were in a building where the Zuzowski family lived. Mr. Zuzowski was a shoemaker. His wife Frania spoke a sophisticated Polish. Her ruddy complexion gave an impression that she was always blushing. They had three children: Roman, a boy my age; a younger sister, Fela, who was painfully shy and spoke only to her own family and me, which lasted until she started first grade; and the youngest boy, Beni, who was a baby when we first moved in. He grew into an adorable blond toddler. His long curly hair cascaded around his attractive face, and he became my favorite object instead of a doll. I dressed him in his sister's dresses and put ribbons in his hair.

Roman attended the first four grades at my Sholom Aleichem School. I connected to him like a brother, and just like siblings, we had our differences and rivalries about grades and games. He was an excellent student and was in direct competition with me. At some point in our rivalry, we even fought physically to the dismay of his parents and my father. When Roman switched schools, the tension between us eased and we were great friends again. Roman and I organized birthday parties for all the children in our building. I solicited our neighbors for candy, cookies, and dishes to make it really festive. The kids helped me with decorations and entertainment. We sang songs, recited poems, and told riddles and jokes.

For the Jewish holiday of Purim, I dressed the building children and myself in our parents' clothes. The masks were created from decorated heavy brown paper. We visited all the Jewish neighbors to collect nuts, candies, or *grosze* (pennies). *"Haint is Purim morgen is oys, gib mir a por groshen und varft mich aroys,"* (Today is Purim, tomorrow it ends, give me a few pennies and throw me out.) This was the customary song that was sung during the Purim door-to-door visits to show off our costumes and appeal for goodies.

Many neighbors depended on me to run to the corner store. Despite the long lines for food, I always was successful in getting ahead in line. I appealed to the kindness of the nearest person in line, telling a sad story of a sick elderly lady I was shopping for.

I was enlisted for babysitting duties for the Zuzowski children, and of course, I did it gladly and for free. I became part of their family. I even joined them on summer vacations in the city of Zarki, in an apartment which they rented from season to season. My absence was a relief for my father and stepmother who didn't want to be bothered with a child on their vacations in the city of Sopot.

Going to and from school, my friends and I stayed together on the tram. We talked and laughed loudly, pushing along with our elbows as we fought our way to get off the crowded tram. When the tram was late, we were happy to see that some teachers were late too. Coming back home on the tram, we usually talked noisily of the events of the day. Sometimes the passengers would make anti-Semitic remarks that Jewish kids made more noise than others. The school we attended could be identified by our uniforms and the initials on our berets.

Sometimes, on the way to or from school, we were taunted and stoned by Polish school children who jeered *"Zydy do Palestyny"* (Jews go to Palestine). They even tried to start a fire in the school basement. It scared some parents who withdrew their children from our school and placed them in the neighborhood Polish school.

Slowly our city was emerging out of the war ruins, and new neighborhoods were built for the workers. The apartments offered a sub-standard life, which was all that a war-torn nation like Poland could provide with their stagnant economy. The ongoing joke was that when one turns on a light, the water runs from the faucet.

Father loved to be seen with pretty, elegant women. He himself had a flair for fashion. His good looks, dark suntanned complexion, black wavy hair touched with a sprinkling of gray, and his blue eyes made him a handsome figure. When he was dressed in his suit for the holidays, women turned their heads to give him a second look.

He was completely blinded by Cyvia, whom he worshiped. I still don't understand, and I'm not alone. Why Cyvia? He used to say that when she strolled down the avenue, her personality and elegant looks brightened the street.

It used to gall Aunt Zosia, who remarked to me, "Has he lost his mind? Did he forget how gracious and beautiful your mother was?" She told me that all the sisters called my mother "the aristocrat."

It pleased me to hear this and connected me more to her, since it was the nickname that Mr. Brandes tacked on to me at school.

Aunt Zosia was witty and had an unusual sense of humor, but it was lost on most occasions because of her devotion and worship with the Jehovah's Witnesses. I loved my aunt very much until I witnessed her punishing her sons by spanking them mercilessly, almost like Grandpa Maj. She swore like a drunken sailor at her family, including Uncle Janek. She even gave him a nickname *"kapusciana glowa"* (cabbage head). This contradiction of the unexpected behavior of a Jehovah's Witness confounded me.

I often walked home from school passing by Father's place of work in order to share with him my displeasure with the results of the day's exams. His workbench stood at a large window from which he looked out for me. He proudly introduced me to his colleagues, boasting about my scholastic achievements and was never fooled by my sad face. He knew it was only an act. He beamed with self-satisfaction when he examined my grades.

Father always regretted that his own education was cut short. His keen mind and curiosity enabled him to develop knowledge and appreciation in many areas, especially classical music. He knew most of the famous operatic arias by heart, but his voice did not match his musical appreciation. Our radio was always tuned to the classical stations, which at times, was a problem for a teenager.

Father's great pleasure was to attend the Wroclaw Opera. He always managed to get the best seats in the house—first balcony center. When Father and Cyvia included me, these experiences instilled in me an appreciation and love of operas and operettas.

14

WARSAW: MY GRADUATION TRIP

As required, all the national Communist holidays were celebrated at our school. The teachers' dictated rules had to be obeyed. The Pioneer uniform of a red bandanna, white blouse, and dark skirt or pants for boys, was a standard attire for those days. The students gathered in the hall of the top floor, where the assembled had to listen to indoctrinating speeches given by the student leadership that bore us to sleep .

The best and most unrestrained party was when we graduated from the Sholom Aleichem School in 1954. The teachers prepared our artistic program, and the parents contributed refreshments and cakes. The gift for our graduation was a trip to our capitol city, Warsaw. The train ride and being together with my schoolmates made the hours fly. It was a known fact that Warsaw was completely destroyed during the war. This was evident by the beehive activity all around and in the reconstruction and rebirth of many tall buildings. Even the hotel, where we stayed overnight, was in the midst of reconstruction.

The Old Town Market was freshly rebuilt in the traditional architecture that was duplicated from old photographs, since the blueprints were lost during the Nazi bombing.

We visited the Jewish Community Center, museum, and the monument of the Warsaw Ghetto Uprising, where we laid a garland of flowers. We were taken to the print shop and office of the famous

Jewish newspaper *Folk Sztyme* (the Voice of the People) It championed the same Communist propaganda as the other newspapers.

Our school picture, which stated that we were the future of Poland, appeared in the paper. Life for us was still calm and simple. Some of my classmates transferred to trade schools but most stayed, attending the Sholom Aleichem High-School.

On Wlodkowicza Street in Wroclaw stood the only open synagogue. People who came to pray were looked upon as traitors or public enemies of Communism, since religion was considered the opium of the people. This anti-religious attitude was ignored by many.

Cyvia insisted that Father not go to work and I skip school on Jewish high holidays like, *Rosh Hashanah*, (Jewish New Year), or *Yom Kippur*, (the Day of Atonement). I was usually given a written excuse from Father to stay home, claiming that I was sick.

A handful of students met in the courtyard of the synagogue that miraculously survived the last days of the War. It was the only synagogue to have survived in Wroclaw. Jews who had lived here for centuries, under the German Empire, built it. For hundreds of years, Wroclaw and most of the western part of Poland belonged to the German Empire.

When I inquired if Mother had been religious, Father told me that she observed the Sabbath and ran a kosher home. Mother's parents were religious (*Cohanim*), belonging to the priestly tribe, who in biblical times served the great temple in Jerusalem. This tribal connection was a birth right inherited through the Father.

Father shared an experience and embarrassment that occurred to him before the war. It was Sabbath, and while Mother was not home, Father acted as a truant child and lit a cigarette. When she surprised him, returning home earlier than expected, he stuck the hot cigarette in his pants pocket. As he was walking toward her, his pants started to smoke, and his indiscretion was discovered. Mother was very upset and disappointed and demanded that Father obey the Sabbath as most Jews do.

The restored Wroclaw Synagogue (photo ©Lerner Vadim/shutterstock.com)

He described how Mother always wore a headscarf in public as a sign of modesty as most religious women did in those days. She was humble, a good homemaker, and a good mother. Father honored her for the dignity and respect that she gave and earned in the community. She was greatly respected by her parents and sisters and was instrumental in promoting and providing our home for Aunt Roma and Uncle Joe Isaac's marriage a few weeks before Adam and I were born. Uncle Joe remembered the happy day and another festive occasion of my brother's circumcision.

Mother's siblings split into two groups—some kept the traditions. Mother belonged to that group, while others, with the influence of the big city, became free thinkers and were the ones who married out of their faith, like Aunts Zosia and Sabina.

Wroclaw also had an established Jewish Culture Club that attracted young and old for daily activities. It housed a small library and snack bar. People played checkers, chess, and ping pong. One of the rooms was reserved for young people to dance to the music of a record player.

The club was where we met our friends and parents, and its popularity, it even enticed non-Jews.

When Ala Szerman, my other classmate, moved on Stalin Street, we became close friends and spent many hours working on our homework together. Her parents welcomed me as if I was a member of the family. I, in turn, became attached to the family. Even the baby sister, Hanusia, became beloved to me, as if she was my little sister.

Mr. Maks Szerman was a stern, serious man, who was respected by his conduct and presence. He was excellent in math, and even though he lacked a formal education, he was able to assist Ala and me with complicated homework. Ala's mother, who was aware of my hard life at the hands of my stepmother, was most kind to me. She served as a cook for our school cafeteria for many years and made sure I ate well.

I told Mrs. Szerman that when I came home and asked Cyvia what I could smear on my bread, her answer was, "Your tongue!"

Mrs. Szerman was a formidable woman who finally confronted Father about the way Cyvia was treating me. But since he did not want to argue with Mrs. Szerman or Cyvia, things remained the same. It appeared that Father was afraid of the neurotic behavior of my stepmother.

Daily, she cried and screamed and carried on about the chimney smoke from the crematoria of Auschwitz. Her mood swings varied from minute to minute. As a child, not knowing the truth of what happened in the Holocaust, her behavior seemed abhorrent to me. It became a harsh ordeal for me since I knew that she could not tolerate me. Of course, the feeling was mutual. At the beginning, when Cyvia became my substitute mother, I had hoped she would treat me like Jozefa, but that was not to be. In the heat of hateful arguments, I continued to beg Father to let me return to Jozefa. Later when a Jewish orphanage became attached to my school, I pleaded with him to let me live there.

15

MY TEENAGE YEARS

The Jewish community was abuzz with news that the borders would soon be opened for those who wanted to go to Israel. At thesame time, my crush, Murzynek, learned that he would be leaving for his homeland, Macedonia. The thought of being parted from him greatly affected me, and I cried from a broken heart. This feeling of loss that subconsciously, I always felt, surfaced with painful sorrow. I could not deal with these unbearable feelings. I escaped by shutting myself off and avoiding him, so that I would not have to say goodbye.

Ida, age 17

Father was relieved when my friendship with Achilles (*Murzynek*) ended. He threatened that if I went out with gentile boys, he would disown me. He dictated, "Don't shame me."

This message was repeated to me by many of my teachers, and even by our school director who respected me for my scholastic achievements. The idea of datingsomeone not Jewish was strongly discouraged. I had yet to learn why.

16

GOODBYE MOTHER JOZEFA

In 1953 the Soviet dictator, Joseph Stalin, died suddenly. Rumors were circulating that he was poisoned. It was the beginning of a new era for the Communist world. The biggest impact was felt in Poland when Wladyslaw Gomulka, one of the Polish anti-Communist leaders, who had been jailed for many years, became the next President. The changes that followed opened up the borders and opportunities for Jews to immigrate to Israel and other countries.

One day, when I came home from school, to my delight, I discovered that we were one of the lucky families allowed to leave Poland. At the office of the Jewish Committee, our name was on the list of those given permission to immigrate to Israel. In the ensuing months, the excitement of going to a far-off, exotic land, Israel, gave us a sense of hope. We seemed to walk with more security and prouder steps.

To us Israel was the land of heroes, who won independence and overcame masses of onslaughts by the surrounding Arab countries. These victories instilled a pride that we were not the forgotten remnants of the Holocaust. We belonged to a heroic people with an ancient history and laws.

My friends were leaving daily. Our goodbyes at the train station were both happy and sad because of the separation as well as leaving the only country we called our homeland. Yet, the expectancy and excitement of the unknown and an open door to the whole world made everyone dream of a life full of freedom, choices, and glitter as seen in the Hollywood movies.

Our family, as many others, made arrangements to get passports and slowly began to sell the possessions that could not be taken along. I was sent on many errands to all kinds of government agencies to get our papers organized for our departure.

At the passport office, a clerk who dealt with Jews daily, asked me if I really felt unsafe and not welcome in Poland. I told him that I personally did not have bad experiences. Frightfully and lately anti-Semitism was growing. A gruesome incident made us scared to stay and gave us a feeling that this was not a country for Jews. An incident that frightened us all was the murder of a young Jewish couple whose bodies were found in the Odra River. The woman was raped and both were beaten to death. They left two small children who later were sent to Israel to join their relatives. The other incident that frightened me was when my friend Ala Szerman and her mother were sprayed with acid as they were walking on the street and speaking Yiddish.

I don't know if the clerk understood or even knew what Jews suffered for centuries in this part of the world. The Final Solution, the Holocaust, destroyed trust and an ability to feel that the country of our birthplace was our home. For me personally, this was a sad realization of the current anti-Semitism because I was saved, with love, by my dear Polish mother.

My stepmother finally came to life when she started to sell our household items, and buy things of value to take to Israel. Our apartment became a beehive of activity with dressmakers who were sewing a wardrobe for Cyvia and comforters for all of us. The luxurious comforters were made of Chinese damask silk, filled with goose down that was floating all over the apartment and in everyone's hair. Too bad we didn't have those warm blankets before; there were so many cold nights that we could have used them.

Among the things that Father purchased were two bicycles. This troubled me because my whole growing years, I did not have one like the other children. I looked at the bikes with a hope that maybe in Israel things would change for me. But the worst blow came when they decided to buy a piano to sell in Israel. All this time, I had dreamed of having one, like the one Grandpa Maj brought from the Jewish ghetto in Czestochowa—the one on which I was given lessons by a neighbor. I squashed my reality and hurt as I recognized that my father and Cyvia did not nurture my childhood with love. I knew what love was like. My mother, Jozefa, had embraced me as her child with tenderness. Often, I questioned my reality in the hands of a hateful stepmother and a weak father who did not protect me.

Carpenters were hired to build huge crates that were to be used for the furniture we were taking to Israel. They filled up all the space in our living room. The apartment looked like a warehouse.

My classmates Ala Szerman and her cousin David Krybus were going to Brazil where their parents had relatives. My stepmother immediately filled Father's head with the idea to send me to Brazil. He wrote a letter to Aunt Sonia, asking if perhaps she would take me to live with her. He suggested that she could take me from the transport heading to Israel in Vienna. The immigrants were to change trains there to go to Genoa, Italy, and then board a ship on the Mediterranean to continue to Israel.

In response to this letter, Sonia replied that as it happened, her business partner's parents lived in Vienna. They would pick me up from the train station with a visa, ready to go to Brazil. My hopes of having a home where I would be welcome made me glad and excited with the promise of being with my kind and generous aunt.

Finally, the time came for us to depart. I took my last train trip to Czestochowa to spend some time with my Polish family. I was invited by my old boyfriend Tozik to join him and his friends at a New Year's celebration dance. They were older students, and I felt excited and grown up to be in their company. When I returned the following day to Mother Jozefa's, she was subdued and sad. She helped me pack and accompanied me to the train station. As we were walking side by side, our time together was spent crying. I promised that I would never forget her, and I would write her often.

The train started to slowly pull away from the station. With tears flowing down my face, I waved at my dear Jozefa as I saw her running after the train, just like the day that she lost me during the war. This time I was leaving her behind.

17

IMMIGRATION

We left Wroclaw for Warsaw where many immigrants gathered for their next leg to Israel. The plan for me to go Brazil was that I would leave our train through an open window of our compartment. Of course, my stepmother was in rapture with the possibility of finally getting rid of me.

We took a train from Warsaw to Czechoslovakia and continued to Austria. Before the train left Warsaw, the immigrating families gathered all our Polish currency to give it to the Polish customs inspector as a bribe to prevent any harassment. The payoff worked, and no one was bothered by the official. He departed with a big grin on his face.

When we arrived in Vienna, my family's hope was shattered when none of the visa papers that my aunt was to have prepared were waiting for me. My aunt's friends, waiting at the train station, told me that the Austrian government was not able to get the papers ready because of the influx of refugees from Hungary caused by the uprising. Their offices were in overload.

My family had only one passport for the three of us and had to surrender it to the delegate of the Israeli agency *Sochnut*, who were taking care of the immigrants and guiding their safe transport. We tried to call Aunt Sonia, but we were not successful in getting through.

Vienna was a completely different world from anything I had ever seen before. I had heard of the Western World, but the pictures were not real in my head until I actually saw with my own eyes. The buildings were in excellent condition. Streets were clean. Flowers were blooming everywhere in vast parks. The stores were filled with merchandise, and the windows displayed their goods in appealing settings. Elegantly dressed people walked about in a leisurely manner. Their faces had a look of happy contentment, not like the stressed people in Poland.

People carried beautifully wrapped packages in shopping bags that looked too fine to just carry their purchases. In Vienna, one could choose whatever was needed or wanted in any store and feel secure that there would be more on other shopping occasions. In Poland, people used and reused battered shopping bags and stood in long lines for whatever they could possibly buy in any store. One bought what was available.

Toward the evening, we had to return to the train. When Father saw me returning, his face turned white while my stepmother started to cry. I was told later that when the leader of the *Sochnut* agency discovered me missing, he lectured Father in a loud angry voice for everyone to hear. "A Father like you will have no one to say *Kaddish* (mourner's prayer) after you die. A Father like you who found his one surviving child after the Holocaust, doesn't deserve a *Kaddish*."

When we boarded the train, my stepmother stopped talking to me and made me stay outside the sleeping compartment. I offered Father and Cyvia some oranges and candy, but she rejected my offer and Father was afraid to speak up. I stood in the corridor all night looking out the window at the beautiful Alps, the many glistening lights and flickering neon signs as we passed cities and villages. The world here was bright in spite of my aching heart.

The next day we arrived in Genoa. As the Italian custom officials were opening a few people's luggage, they pointed to a man, instructing him to open his suitcase. The only possessions that this man had was a portrait of his old *Chassidic* parents and an aluminum cooking pot. This scene, this poor man, and my own distraught emotional state, brought me to tears. This incident caused the inspectors to become agitated, and appearing saddened and embarrassed, they stopped searching through the immigrants' luggage.

Our sojourn in Celle Ligure, Italy, was short. From here, we were bussed to Genoa where we boarded an Italian boat to Israel. Many of the travelers, including Cyvia, were seasick the entire voyage. Father and I went alone to the dining room and enjoyed the plentiful fare. It was a carefree time, just dreaming of what awaited us in Israel and how we would adjust to a new life, new language, and new country.

The unusually warm weather made the journey seem longer than the few days it was to be. The view of the Greek Islands was intriguing and brought to mind the bewitching mythological stories and history.

18

ISRAEL

As we approached the skyline of Israel, from a distance, we were able to discern glistening white houses, perched on a mountain, set against the bluest sky I had ever seen. My idea of what Israel would look like came from postcards that relatives sent us for *Rosh Hashanah*. The cards showed Arabs walking with camels in the desert sand. I was in awe of the view of a modern, beautiful city that stretched as far as the eyes could see.

On a beautiful day in April 1957, we arrived in the Port of Haifa. My Uncle Gedalie, who could have been mistaken for Father's twin, and his wife, Ester, met us at the port. They had immigrated a few years before—soon after their miraculous survival in Auschwitz. She gave me directions on how to get to her house, which was close to the port. When I left the boat, my parents remained to look after the luggage and crates and inquire with customs what duty would be needed to be paid.

The *Sochnut* assigned us to an area readied for immigrants called *Maabarah* (temporary housing in the Valley of Beitch*an*), which was sometimes made of asbestos and sheet metal. These areas were settled with new arrivals for a couple of reasons—to settle the land by Jews and act as a shield on the borders of unfriendly Arab states.

As I walked to Aunt Ester's house, I stopped to ask a storekeeper for directions in Yiddish, "Do you know Yiddish?"

"Yes, for a nice blonde girl, I know Yiddish," he replied.

Ida and a Camel, Israel 1957

When I stopped at another place, I heard the same reaction, "What a pretty blonde."

I was taken aback by all the comments and thought to myself that it must be something special to be blonde in Israel. As I met other people, they too looked with smiling kind stares. Everywhere I went people were friendly and helpful. I began to feel a love and a bond with this Jewish land—the nation of Israel. Exhilarated and with great pride, tears of joy flowed when I realized that this was my homeland. I had come home!

Aunt Ester, Uncle Gedalie, and their two daughters shared a fifty-year-old abandoned Arab house with two other families. It was a traditional Arabic stone structure with columns supporting it. The mosaic tile floors added character and color. It was a pretty building. The exotic architecture brought to mind the stories of Ali Baba or other great tales about the Islamic world.

Haifa was essentially made up of three levels, starting at the Mediterranean and climbing up the sides of Mount Carmel. The first level was the port itself and streets full of stores, small industry, and Arab private buildings. The second level was dotted with structures, mixed with old and modern buildings. Sometimes they were cantilevered on stilts against the mountainside. At the top was the most prestigious neighborhood called Carmel with large, luxurious homes and condominiums. The view was breathtaking, especially at night. The lights from the port joined the stars in the sky and blended together like sparkling crystals on a soft velvet cloth. In the daytime, one could see the whole city below and the city of Akko across the beach.

Immediately, I fell in love with Israel and its warm, friendly people who felt like family. Everywhere I went, on the bus or street, when I tried to speak Hebrew, people would kindly correct me. All were eager for the newcomers to learn Hebrew quickly. That was followed by the usual question—where I was from—and trying to figure out if possibly I may be related. After a while, I came to understand that everyone was still looking for lost family from the war.

I did meet some people who claimed me as family. Such a thought started to make me wonder seriously about possible connections. People were finding each other just by chance. I heard about women, from my city in Poland, who found either husbands, a child, or members of their family.

Another miracle happened when my friend went to a kibbutz to study Hebrew. Somebody noticed that she strongly resembled a woman who cooked in the kitchen. It turned out to be her long-lost mother. One heard of such stories every day. These miracles were happening around me, which sparked hope that both amazed and unnerved me and made me feel restless. Inside I felt as if there was something or someone who was waiting for me, looking for me.

Right from the beginning I thought, *Oh my God, what if in one of the kibbutzim I would find my twin brother Adam and sister Gienia?* With hope and anticipation, I, too, started questioning people I met about their names and the places they came from. I searched through the telephone books for our family names.

I asked Uncle Gedalie, "Did you hear about any other Paluchs here in Israel? Did you look around to find family?"

Uncle Gedalie always looked very sad and only shook his head. I could not discern if it meant yes or no. Gedalie was greatly affected by the Holocaust and carried the burden of the martyred victims. He seldom smiled. He established a new family, but his loss during the Holocaust was on his mind and showed on his tired face. Like other

Ida, Israel 1957

survivors, he felt guilty that he survived.

He married Aunt Ester immediately after the war in a DP camp in Germany where they met. Their first daughter, Jona, was born there. They came to Israel and established new roots, a new life in Haifa. Though Aunt Ester was also a Holocaust survivor from Auschwitz, she was the opposite of my stepmother. She was cheerful, positive thinking, and full of energy. She taught me things I never learned from my stepmother—how to wash and iron clothes, how to keep things orderly and neat. Everything was told with humor and a smile.

When I moved in with them, Jona was a teenager and Gitale, who was born in Haifa, was about five years old. I wanted to be part of this family and indeed started to feel like one of them. Aunt Ester treated me like one of her daughters.

At that time, Israeli residents had ration cards. It was a time called *tzena*, meaning that some foods were scarce and rationed. Only through those coupons one could buy things like sugar and chocolate for their families. Aunt Ester never differentiated between me and her children and shared everything including her daughters' chocolate allotment. My rationing card was kept by Cyvia and Father in Beitchan.

On the first night with my Israeli family, Uncle Gedalie took me out to eat falafel. He wanted to make sure that I knew how to appreciate and get the full taste of falafel as the *Sabras* (persons born in Israel) enjoyed. As customary, he poured hot sauce all over it. The spicy foods were new to me and I could not appreciate nor tolerate them. I was coughing and trying to get rid of the taste all the way home. I declared that I would never touch falafel again. When the neighbors learned about my aversion and reaction to falafel, they gleefully boasted, "Just you wait. You'll see. You'll develop a taste for it yet."

This prediction came true sooner than I thought. In no time, it became my favorite treat. Even today, when I go to Israel, the first thing I do is stop to indulge at a falafel place.

A few months after our arrival, Father and Cyvia had a chance to get out of Beitchan. She had two older brothers and an uncle in Hajfa, who came to Israel with the Zionist movement before World War II. She was able to get a one room apartment in Tel Aviv from her rich uncle in his ice factory. Immediately, Cyvia declared that there was no room for me. My hurt feelings knew that there would be room for ten children if they were hers. Of course, for the sake of peace, Father, as usual, did not take a stand to protect his own child.

Uncle's family embraced me with open arms, and their love became very dear to me. My two cousins were happy to have an older cousin living with them. Jona, a very serious teenager for her age, looked just like her mother. Tova, a delightful five-year-old, looked a little like me and stuck to me like glue. She asked me to comb her blonde hair in a ponytail and spoke to me the sweetest Hebrew words I had ever heard. She asked me to walk her to play school, and on the way, she kissed my hands. I stayed with Uncle Gedalie's family for almost two months, and although it was very hard for them, I never heard them complain or even suggest that I leave.

I followed the advice from other immigrants that the *Sochnut* could enroll me in a kibbutz where I could study Hebrew in exchange for work. Within a short time, I was informed that there was room for me at one of the nicest kibbutzim in the country, called Geva in the Galil, not far from Afula and Nazareth. It looked like a quaint little village where everyone had their own modest housing and at the center stood a school and library.

The grounds were covered with a profusion of flowers and giant roses. Kibbutz Geva's industry was growing roses, grapes, and raising fish in a fresh-water pond. It was a beautiful serene place, with a view of the Gilboa Mountains that inspired daydreaming and tender feelings.

Every evening, movies were shown on a large outdoor screen. We sat on the grass, under skies full of stars, together with the kibbutz members, who relaxed after a hard day's work. I saw almost all of the Doris Day films, and the famous musical "Seven Brides for Seven Brothers." The Elvis Presley movies were a wonderful delight to me, since I was already familiar with his music from Poland. The films were in English, with Hebrew subtitles. After a few weeks, I understood most of the dialogue. I found this to be an enjoyable way to reinforce my knowledge of Hebrew because the same movies were shown over and over again. In addition, visiting folk-singing groups and musicians from other kibbutzim came often to entertain us.

The members of the kibbutz were mostly from Russia. They came to Israel with revolutionary ideology and were well-educated. They didn't mind working in the fields, in the kitchen, or with cows or chickens. For the first time, I saw a mechanized chicken coop where the eggs rolled out on automated assembly lines. Medical and dental care was available to all the members of the kibbutz, and many other opportunities were given to all for an improved life.

Some of my schoolmates and teachers also came to learn Hebrew. It seemed suspicious that some teachers learned Hebrew so quickly. When I asked them about it, they explained that many of these teachers knew Hebrew from before the war. They once belonged to Zionist organizations, attended *yeshivas*, (religious schools for boys), and were the generation who tried to revive Hebrew as a modern language. They looked at Israel as the past and the future for the Jewish people. But the Holocaust stopped all their dreams. Those living under the Communists were discouraged from such activities and gave up the ideals that they once yearned for.

In the Ulpan, I shared a room with another girl. The housing was called *tzrifim* (a sort of cabin made of wood and aluminum.) The toilet facility was an outhouse situated at a distance, at the end of a group of cabins. Boys and girls had separate quarters, and individual housing was supplied for married couples with children. The immigrants were from all over Iraq, Iran, Morocco, Egypt, Hungary, and other countries. I stood out with my blonde hair, but to me, they were the ones who had exotic looks.

When I saw a group of youngsters from India, I asked the kibbutz members, "Are they Jews too? They don't look like Jews."

I had never seen such a variety of cultures and different people in my whole life.

I said to them, "You're not Jewish." They replied back, "You're not Jewish."

They followed up, "We are the real Jews!" I replied, "Oh no, you are Indian!"

The argumentation continued, but somehow, we all grew to love each other and found that we did have much in common. We were all about the same age and eagerly studied Hebrew. We shared the same plight of being discriminated against in our native countries. I made friends with everyone.

Often, I came face to face with snakes, tarantulas, and large flying bugs when I was assigned to work in the fields. I soon got used to them and overcame the shock.

The first word that I learned in Hebrew was *shilshul* (diarrhea) because it became my affliction. It was probably due to the new environment, new food, and the relentless heat. Having a light complexion and green eyes, the sun was hard on me. It was difficult for me to be outdoors for long periods of time because of my recurring migraine headaches.

My clothing also was not ideal for the hot Israeli weather. As they say, necessity is the mother of invention. I cut my pumps around leaving only the soles. I sewed little rings on them, put ribbons through, tied the ribbons across my feet, and created my own sandals.

To my delight, the kibbutz gave me work clothes. The green shorts and blouses with tiny white and green checkered designs that were new, neat, pressed, and fit me, making me feel that I finally fit in. I looked like one of them, and it gave me a sense of belonging.

Eventually, my homemade sandals wore out and the kibbutz gave me new ones.

In the meantime, I blossomed into a woman's figure and was even supplied with bras. Everything was supplied by the kibbutz, including cigarettes, even though I was not a smoker. I gave them to people who smoked.

Everybody looked suntanned and healthy from laboring in the outdoors. Life in the kibbutz was good, and I was content. The members were caring and warm toward us. Sometimes they asked me where I was from, and when they learned that I was from Poland, they wanted to hear how I had survived. My story must have touched them for they showed a special caring attention to me.

My roommate was a Hungarian girl, a few years older and more mature. When her sailor boyfriend came to visit, bringing gifts, she asked me to leave the room. I did not understand why until the other girls educated me. At age seventeen, I was inexperienced and naive.

I was at an age to either get married or join the army. Very few people from our Ulpan made a love connection at the kibbutz and got married. The ones who chose the army did better in life than the ones who got married just to escape service. They were the lucky ones that acquired maturity and schooling through the army. Most of my girlfriends who joined the army were trained in nursing.

Right from the start I learned how compassionate the kibbutz members were toward the newcomers. The first time we were driven in a truck to the vegetable fields, we wore special hats, called *kova tembel*. They looked like safari hats but the linen material was not as thick. Early in the morning, we arrived at the field to weed the vegetables. When the sun rose high in the sky, I felt that the heat would kill me. My face turned beet red, followed by a bloody nose and a severe headache.

Since we were too far from the kibbutz to take me back, a member, who supervised us, said to me, "Judith, (my new Hebrew name) sit down in the shade under that tree. You will return to work when the sun goes down."

I gladly sat in the shade where I was pampered with lunch and water, while I waited for the sun to set. As the sun was disappearing, I declared that I was ready to work, but the man said, "Go home."

The next day they arranged for me to work indoors. I was assigned to the laundry to iron shirts—mountains of shirts. Having no experience, a woman in charge showed me the step by step process, and I was left to my assignment. I ironed and ironed until I was exhausted but the pile decreased, although in the process I scorched a few shirts. When the woman came back to check on me, she found chaos in the laundry room.

Shaking her head in disbelief she said, "No, you don't fit here." I was moved to the kitchen, where I washed mountains of dishes.

I was stationed to work next to a handsome Hungarian boy who was unattached. After work the boy invited me to meet his parents. He showed me his albums of photographs of himself and his life in Hungary. We found that we had much in common since we both came from Communist countries. We became friends.

My next assignment was to babysit children in the kibbutz. They had their own quarters, without their parents, and slept together in groups according to their ages. This job I liked best. The children were friendly innocent and curious. They were about five and six years old, and asked me in the sweetest little voices, "What's your name?"

They wanted me to tell them stories, but I couldn't because I didn't speak enough Hebrew yet. Working with the youngsters made me think of my own life. I was so alone. My veiled memories cropped up about my twin brother and older sister. I would even fantasize at times that these children were my siblings. I was always looking into peoples' faces, wondering if they possibly could be my brother or sister. What is your name? Where did you come from? What country? What city? These questions were always on my mind and often asked.

Sometimes a group of young people ventured to an open movie theater to see American films. Everyone around was nibbling on different seeds—sunflower, pumpkin, or peanuts—and spitting or throwing the shells on the ground. It seemed to me like a crude way of behaving, yet I admired the defiant, strong spirit that was exhibited, especially by the *sabras*. Surround by this extraordinary population, I did not know what to think. I wanted so to be like them, sure and safe.

The evening air was fresh and when one gazed up at the sky, the millions of stars were winking down as if approving and protecting us. The air-conditioned theaters of today could never equal the special feeling of the outdoors at the kibbutz.

My carefree life without worries had to come to an end. I knew that my stay at the kibbutz would be over within weeks. I started to think what to do and to whom to turn. Meanwhile, my mother's sister Aunt Zosia and Uncle Janek ended up living in the *Maabara* (transit settlement) in the city of Lod in a *tzrif* (a cabin). Uncle Janek got a very good job with El Al Airlines since he was an excellent toolmaker. The area was set up with temporary housing with outhouses at the end of the row of the cabins. These quarters were unbearably hot in the summer and cold in the winter. Each was equipped with a kerosene cooking stove, a kitchen, a shower room, and one large room where four beds stood on a stone floor. Eventually the settlement was developed with permanent housing.

The area was surrounded with wild cactuses and olive trees. At night one heard the howling wild animals, and in the daytime slithering snakes terrified the new immigrants. The closest market place was in *Ramla,* where we shopped for vegetables and pitas, and where most of the population was Arab.

Aunt Zosia and Uncle Janek left Poland for Germany in 1946. In Berlin, wanting desperately to find herself, Zosia joined the Jehovah's Witnesses, which developed into a dedication and an obsession of spreading their beliefs. Aunt Zosia was an insecure woman. This arose from the fact that after the war, when she and Uncle Janek, her Polish common-law husband, came out of hiding, many looked down on her. Even her own sisters disapproved, forgetting that her husband had saved her life.

When Zosia, Janek, and their two children immigrated to Israel, she continued to belong to Jehovah's Witnesses and preached all over Lod and the adjoining settlements. Uncle Janek was an easy-going person and never joined in her beliefs, although he did not condemn her for her newly-found religion. He stuck to his own beliefs. Janek let Zosia do whatever she wanted as long as he could live in peace. Their two sons, Bogdan and Stefan, attended an Israeli school soon after arriving, and within a few months they spoke Hebrew and were absorbed into Israeli life.

Aunt Zosia fixed up her little *tzrif* into an orderly, clean dollhouse. She placed a rug on the floor and displayed her crystal objects to enhance the usually drab surroundings. Everyone around came to see and take an example of how to set up their own places.

On many occasions, I hitchhiked to *Maabara* from the kibbutz, not fearing any danger. Every time that I was picked up, as usual,   I was asked the same questions to see if possibly, we might be related. The hope of finding a missing relative or friend was a constant quest. I made many friends in my hitchhiking travels, and sometimes they waited for me the following week to take me to   my aunt's again. People were easy going and helpful. Doors were never locked and fear of thievery was non-existent.

Because of the underlying hostility between her and her sister Roma, who was living in Chicago and wouldn't sponsor her to come to the States, Aunt Zosia devised another plan. She came to visit me a few times at the kibbutz. Her underlying errand and intent was to marry me off to a rich tourist from the United States. Then when I settled in the States, I could sponsor her family to come to America. In the meantime, she hoped and expected to earn a matchmaking fee from the prospective groom.

Aunt Zosia came to the kibbutz every week and each time introduced me to someone new. If I did not like her choice, she ridiculed and criticized me for my looks, especially my thin hair and flat chest. Zosia used scare tactics, saying that the girls who joined the Israeli army were taken advantage of by the male soldiers. To add to my insecurities, Father did not bother to visit me at the kibbutz. This confirmed that he and my stepmother didn't care for me, nor would I be welcome in their home. I felt completely abandoned.

It appeared to me that Zosia was the only person who showed interest in me, and I started to listen to her advice and guidance. I was too naive to understand her selfish manipulation. On one of the visits, she took me to Tel Aviv where she arranged a meeting with an American tourist from New York. He came for the precise reason of finding a wife. He was a Holocaust survivor from Poland. His looks and uncultured, crude manners and expressions turned me off. No matter what my aunt said, she could not persuade   me to accept such a man as a husband. That was not the future I dreamed of at age seventeen.

19

ON MY OWN

My stay in Kibbutz *Geva* was coming to an end, since it was only a temporary stay to study Hebrew. I could not become a member—it was very complicated. I left and went to the beautiful city of Netanya where my mother's cousin Guta lived. Guta and her husband Shmuel left Poland just before the German occupation. They were avid Zionists and fulfilled their dream to resettle and rebuild the Holy Land.

Netanya was a tourist destination where people came to enjoy the golden sand beaches and stroll about in the extensive rose gardens and parks located by the beach. I walked there to escape my ugly moods, and on many occasions, would meet people who spoke Polish.

I made friends with a sister and brother whose mother was Polish and their father a Jew. She saved their father during the war. As I got to know them, I found out that Bronia and her brother were twins and were born about the same time as I was. Seeing their camaraderie and closeness made me envious and sparked a longing for my lost brother, Adam.

Bronia wanted out of Israel and purposefully dated tourists. She met an older Jewish man from Germany and convinced her mother to officially convert to Judaism in order to be able to marry him. The law of Israel stated that only a proven Jew may get a marriage certificate from the Rabbinical Orthodox Authority. Religion is passed on through a mother.

Bronia took me under her wing and showed me the attractions of the city. When she shot all the film in her camera, we went to her friend Zvi Stein's photo studio to have the film processed. He was an attractive man, of medium build with sad black, almond shaped eyes and black hair with a slight hint of gray at the temples.

He greeted us cheerfully and I detected an intimacy between them. As we sat in his studio and started to chat, he stared at me with curiosity. When I returned to pick up the processed pictures for Bronia, Zvi seemed interested in my past and in me. For the first time, since I arrived in Israel, I found myself sharing my uprooted and hurtful life with someone who listened and understood my plight. We talked for a long time until he closed the studio. We continued our conversation walking on the street, him leading his bicycle. He suggested that we get a bite to eat, but first we stopped at his apartment so he could change his clothing.

He had tears in his eyes as he listened to me. He told me about his divorce and the eight-year-old son he had to place with his brother and sister-in-law after his wife took off. We were two anguished souls who opened their hearts and found comfort in each other's platonic embrace. It was an innocent expression of finding some comfort for the sorrow in our lives. I felt as if a burden was lifted off my heart. I was not alone with such an ache. We continued to the sidewalk café. Our conversation continued in the same vain, but somehow, I felt a glimmer of hope that things would improve and get better.

My stay with cousin Guta did not last long since I needed a job, and Netanya was not the place to find one. I decided that Tel Aviv offered more opportunities. Guta gave me an address of my mother's cousin Jadzia. I stayed there a few days. One night, Jadzia called up to me that there was a man asking for me. When I came to the hallway, there stood Zvi. He learned from cousin Guta where I was living. We walked on the beach, and I told him about not having a job or a place to live. His expression of kindness and understanding gave me a feeling that someone did care. He told me that he would stay in touch with me.

I could not stay at Jadzia's, since I was only a guest. In the meantime, I had a big fight with Aunt Zosia and Father, who did not understand why I would not marry a rich tourist. They accused me of being the most stupid and impractical woman on the face of the earth by my refusal to marry an American. They officially disowned me, telling this straight to my face. Again, I felt abandoned with no place to go and no one to advise or offer a kind word. Staying with Jadzia came to an end, and I was again homeless.

With no options, I decided to turn to the immigration office *Sochnut* for help and took the bus to their office. It was late and I was worried that it would be closed by the time I arrived. Apprehensively, I asked a man sitting next to me if this was the stop for the agency. He asked me if I was an *ola hadasha* (a new immigrant). I answered that I was and told him that I needed a safe place to stay overnight. He informed me that he had just arrived from Russia, where he was imprisoned for more than ten years, and was currently staying in a *Beit Halutzot* (apartments for single people).

It was a lucky stroke that I ran into this man. He offered to take me there and introduce me to the management. Not only did he give me good advice that night, but he also arranged a job for me. The next day he took me to his cousin, who was a dressmaker, and told her to take me in as an apprentice. She had a shop in her home and besides me, she had another girl with sewing experience to help her out.

In the beginning, my job was to go to her customers and collect the money due to her. I walked and sometimes took buses in a hundred degrees heat to find them and collect the long overdue money. Some of the customers were always home, while some set their dogs against me in order to scare me away.

I made very little money, not enough to buy food and grew weak. Thankfully, the housing in *Beit Halutzot* was free. No one was allowed to cook inside the dorms, so I had to go to a cafeteria. I sat in a corner so nobody would see my hand shake when I tried to hold a spoon. I was close to a nervous breakdown, but I didn't know the signs or what it meant.

I went on Allenby Street and stopped in stores to inquire for any position as an addition to my job for the seamstress. But I usually was mistaken for a customer. When I explained I was looking for a job, I was politely refused. I felt desperate when I came across an employment agency where many young Jewish girls, from all over the world, all colors and shapes, were looking for jobs. I asked a Moroccan girl to help me fill out an application. She asked me what I could do. I told her that until now, I had never worked professionally and had no experience. She asked me about my hobbies, and I replied that I loved to draw faces and flowers on paper. She took me for a walk and shared her lunch with me.

She told me that the agency sent her to a man that did some art work and maybe he would be able to use my skills. She suggested that I keep this job from the agency in case I get hired, so I wouldn't have to pay them a commission—part of my salary. When we got to the man's apartment, I was hired immediately on the recommendation of the girl.

I started to work every morning in my new boss's home, an immigrant from Romania, who made toys and trinkets. Mostly, he collected old burned-out bulbs, cut them and filled them with water. Then he put little miniature views of landscapes on a base, with pieces of white plastic confetti floating about. He then sealed the bulbs and sold them to different vendors on the streets of Tel Aviv. That job ended when the boss's wife returned from her vacation and did not like my presence in her home. I went back to the dressmaker, who rehired me because she thought that her nephew Alex was my boyfriend.

20

MY OWN FAMILY

My life was a daily struggle that starved my body and soul. My loneliness and isolation brought me down very low and hopeless. After a few months, Zvi found me through Guta. He told me that he cared for me and that marrying him would be a good solution to my problems. I thought that he was too old for me, but he was kind and trustworthy. He was the only person in whom I could talk or confide. We dated for few months, and finally I agreed to marry him.

I went to my father and stepmother to invite them to our wedding ceremony. Father came without Cyvia to Netanya where the wedding ceremony took place in a Rabbi's study. It was arranged with the help of Zvi's sister-in-law Sylvia and his younger brother Jacob.

I agreed to take Zvi's nine-year old son from Sylvia, and raise him as my own. I dreamed of being the perfect stepmother. I would show the world that I would not be like Cyvia. Unfortunately, my new sister-in-law was not crazy about the idea of an eighteen-year-old taking over parenting of Shimon. Sylvia sacrificed a great deal to care for the boy. She even postponed having her own children. Her commitment and love were unwavering. So Zvi and I started our married life in his apartment without his son.

Another newlywed couple were also renting a room from our landlady. They were from Yemen. Tamar and I became good friends, shared recipes, and spent time shopping at the market together. The common kitchen was small, and my culinary skills were limited.

Determined to fit the image of a good wife, I searched out an Israeli cookbook translated to Polish, which was my first step towards becoming a good cook.

Tamar and I had even more in common when we became pregnant at the same time. While I was pregnant, I enrolled in a Hebrew Ulpan Akiva that was popular in our city. When I found out about my pregnancy, I did not know that I was supposed to go to the doctor for a check-up every few weeks. I stopped smoking after finally seeing a doctor, who informed me that smoking is very harmful to the development of the baby.

Tamar and I were a comical pair when we decided to ride on one bike on the streets of Netanya with our big bellies. A policeman stopped us and said with a smile, "Two beauties, one from Poland, the other from Yemen want to smash the bicycle. I don't care, but what about the safety of your babies?"

I was thrilled about becoming a mother and caring for my very own child. From the beginning, I was sure that I was carrying a girl. Most men in Israel wanted sons. The wives were anxious to fulfill their husband's dream with the birth of a boy. Regardless, I only wanted a girl. I wanted to give her my mother's name, Ester, the dearest and only gift I had.

Early Saturday morning, on June 13, 1959, while experiencing some pain, I went to the park where Zvi was working taking pictures. As the pains became worse and closer, we took an ambulance to the hospital in Hadera. The driver of the ambulance wanted to cheer me up and said, "Every pregnant woman that goes in my ambulance delivers a boy."

I immediately countered, "This one is going to be a girl."

Looking around in the waiting room, I felt a sense of relief seeing so many women, including Arab women, trusting the Israeli medical system. I was checked by a young doctor who advised me that I was ready to deliver soon. I was given a shot to speed the labor, but instead I fell asleep.

When I awoke, the young doctor playfully joked that I was a strange woman, "The shot had an opposite effect on you. Where are you from?"

When I told him that I was from Wroclaw, Poland, he asked if I knew Minia Fuks. I told him that she was my first-grade teacher. He was astonished because she was his sweetheart. My baby was not in a hurry to arrive. I wished for the baby to be born and yet was glad of the delay and opportunity to see the process of birth by my companions. The doctor came in the evening and gave me another shot to stimulate the birth. It took less than three oys, ouches, and fifteen minutes, and my baby girl arrived. When I was told it was a girl, I was overjoyed, yet I could not believe that my wish came true. I asked the nurse to check again.

A baby was brought to me that looked more like my neighbor Tamar than me. She had dark skin and a head-full of brown hair, and when she smiled or perhaps grimaced, a dimple formed in her right cheek. Ester looked big for a newborn. She was beautiful and perfect. Ester was my triumph of the love that I missed and was ready to give. I immediately began breastfeeding and even though my bosoms were sore, I did not care. I was happy that she wanted to eat. I held my little one, inspecting every inch of her, admiring in amazement how beautiful she was.

People in our neighborhood upgraded their apartments, and bought new furniture, while we still lived in our small government housing without the prospect of improving our lives. Our photo studio was in the center of town. The main street, Hertzel, snaked along the beach. It seemed as if it was one long outdoor restaurant where people checked each other out as they paraded in their finery. The hotels located along the length of the sandy beach attracted a flood of tourists. The parks, restaurants, and ice-cream parlors were filled with visitors and locals.

The Stein Photo Studio that Zvi and his brother Jacob owned did not generate enough income for two families. My husband thought of opening another studio, maybe in another city, but it never materialized.

My sister-in-law's cousin, Shmuel, who was a longtime friend of Zvi, came to us with a new idea that changed the course of our lives. He told us that he applied at the American Embassy for an immigration visa. Shmuel had a steady job with the Israeli army and could not find employment outside the army. He was a bachelor and hoped to see the world.

Going to the United States was my husband's dream. He asked Shmuel to bring him an application the next time he visited the embassy. Soon Shmuel brought one for us, which we filled out, and he took to the embassy. We never expected that a year later, we would hear from the immigration department asking us to submit the necessary documents if we were still interested in going to the U.S.

I was never enthusiastic about going to America, but Zvi reminded me every day how hard life was for us in Israel. I succumbed to my husband's pressure. But we needed a sponsor from the United States, so Zvi suggested that I write to Aunt Zosia, who had moved to Chicago after her sister Roma sponsored her after all. I felt she should help me since she had created many difficulties in my life. She owed me. Zosia, not being a citizen, could not be a sponsor, but she came up with an idea that maybe one of her fellow Jehovah's Witnesses would help. And indeed, a friend of hers sponsored us.

It took only a few months to get our personal business in order and we were ready to leave. When cousin Guta heard of our plan, she decided to join us. She got a special work visa from relatives in the States that allowed them to leave immediately. We coordinated our voyage on a boat named Israel and arrived together in New York. The day we left Haifa, Father, Uncle Gedalie, his wife, Ester, and both cousins Jona and Tova came to say goodbye.

21

THE LAND OF OPPORTUNITIES AND MIRACLES

My first impression of New York was shocking. Zvi's sister- in-law, Sylvia's aunt, greeted us at the port and took us in a cab, which we paid for, and were told to give a big tip for the driver. A tip was an unusual custom for us because in Israel or Poland tipping was not done.

The aunt lived in an apartment in public housing. On the way to Manhattan, we saw many poor, black people. When we reached our destination, drunk men and woman were lying around on the sidewalks. I was dumbfounded to see such scenes. The scenes of poverty in Poland flashed back here. Where was the pink America of Doris Day? Where were the elegant homes and sophisticated people sipping cocktails that I had seen in the American movies? This must be all a nightmare, but it wasn't. Soon we learned the truth about the American myth of "money growing on trees."

The aunt made sure we rented a hotel room and didn't stay with her. The room had one window and four drab walls. Looking out the window, adjoining building walls were the obstacles that blocked any possibility of a view. It was impossible to open the window for air because a stench shocked one in to closing it immediately. People just tossed their garbage out from their windows, and no one bothered to remove the rot, probably for months.

I felt trapped and depressed, and immediately wanted to go back home to Israel, where everything was bright, the sky was blue, and I felt like my family was safe. But Zvi did not want to hear about going back. He insisted that we had to give it a chance. Besides, we used a loan from the store for our fare to come to America, and our apartment back home was already rented.

The next day, we went downtown where there were some photo studios and inquired about jobs. We had difficulties communicating, but luckily, we found many people who spoke Yiddish. After few days of hotel fees, we started to worry about our finances. We only had one thousand dollars with us, and the money was disappearing quickly. Finally, Guta called us. We told her that Zvi had no luck finding work. She suggested that we come to Coney Island.

She told us that we wouldn't believe where she lived. It was a closed community with a fence, and one had to explain who they were visiting before they were let in. She and her husband where employed by some people who lived in this gated community.

Guta promised that an apartment would cost less than staying in a hotel in New York. So, we took our possessions, which consisted of three large suitcases, and went on a train to Coney Island. Guta met us at the stop, and helped us rent a bedroom from a young Jewish couple with children. They were very sympathetic to our plight. When we were searching for an apartment, we were shocked when we saw signs that said, "No dogs or Jews allowed."

The husband from whom we were able to get a room, drove Zvi around for a few days to help him find work, but they were unsuccessful. In desperation, I called Aunt Zosia in Chicago and asked her what to do. She told me to take the train and come to Chicago. She said that if someone can't find work anywhere, they always find work in Chicago. So, the next day, we bought tickets in a sleeping car that took more than fourteen hours to get there. The noise of the train and the worry about the future kept me up all night.

When we finally arrived in Chicago, we were greeted by Aunt Zosia, Uncle Janek, and their older son, Bogdan. Their apartment on Ashland Avenue, close to the Howard "L" station, was an old-fashioned apartment in an older building. As always, Aunt Zosia's magic was evident. The place was spotless. It was furnished with a combination of old and new furniture, which she and her husband varnished and upholstered to the point that it looked better than in its original state. The house smelled of cooking and baking.

She was excited to see us and meet our daughter, Ester. She told me that she looked like the Romanian, meaning like my husband. She had a most unique sense of humor and had a special talent of giving nicknames to people that were both funny and appropriate to their personality.

Aunt Zosia was still an attractive woman for her age, which she never wanted to reveal. She was anxious to help find a job for Zvi and even more urgently, an apartment for us. The next day, my cousin Bogdan took my husband to Devon Avenue where there were a few photo studios. One did hire Zvi because he knew that he would work for any price.

As soon as Aunt Zosia learned that Zvi got a job, she urged us to move out. We had no idea how to go about it, but she knew the neighborhood, and soon we rented a one-bedroom apartment a few blocks away from her on Paulina Street. The apartment was clean and so was the immense building.

Too soon, we found that Zvi's small earnings were not enough to pay rent and buy food. I immediately started to look for a job. But having no one to care for Ester, I was not free to go to work even if I had succeeded in finding one. I was advised to visit the local HIAS (Hebrew Immigrant Aid Society) which sometimes helped newcomers.

Soon I found out that I belonged to the wrong category of immigrants. HIAS definitely did not help Jews who left Israel. Nevertheless, I tried to explain my situation that I especially needed assistance with daycare for Ester. I was interviewed by a woman who either misunderstood me or was insensitive. She left the room and returned with a lawyer advising me to give up my child for adoption. I got very offended and almost afraid and ran with my child, holding her tight, slamming the door behind me.

22

STRUGGLING IN AMERICA

In my struggle to find a way to help our little family, I decided to attend a free English class for newcomers, held in the evenings, at the local library. The ladies there, also newcomers, who were already experienced about finding ways to survive, told me about a factory that needed unskilled workers in their wrapping department. I went there and was hired immediately on the good recommendations of my new schoolmates.

My next dilemma of how to take advantage of this job forced me to go searching the streets for an answer, pushing Ester in the stroller. I walked the streets for a long time, and just as I was about to return home defeated, I spotted a playschool through a store window.

I went inside to inquire, with my dictionary in hand, and managed to talk to the owner. Mrs. Davis, a middle-aged woman, was listening intently with a friendly expression on her face. She asked me to wait and soon returned with another woman.

Addressing the two of us, "You two ladies are neighbors and have girls the same age, so you have a lot common."

Melita Surlin, also a Holocaust child survivor from Austria, who survived the Holocaust years with her mother in England, knew Yiddish. She was able to translate my predicament to Mrs. Davis. Mrs. Davis immediately and generously proposed that I bring Ester every day to her playschool, and she would wait until I started my job to get paid. The following day I pushed the stroller two miles back and forth to the day care, as I started to work at my job.

The first day I came to pick up Ester, Mrs. Davis presented my child back to me in new, comfortable clothes and sneakers. She looked just like one of the American children in her school. I made friends with some other mothers who kept the children with Mrs. Davis. I was even invited to birthday parties—American style. They were not much different than the ones in Israel.

Our introduction to the Surlin family developed right away into a warm friendship. The girls adopted each other and were good playmates. My husband found a brotherly soul in her husband, Sidney, and his younger brother, George. George and his wife Bessie lived around the corner. They had no children. Both brothers were pharmacists and amateur *chazanim,* (cantors).

As it happens, Zvi had an unfulfilled dream of becoming a famous cantor. He spent large sums of money training his voice in Israel and continued doing so in Chicago, in spite of his lack of voice and money. The only thing that he had going for him was his knowledge of Hebrew and a religious childhood upbringing from Romania.

Shortly after we arrival to Chicago, Zosia surprised me with a family photograph of my mother holding my twin brother Adam and me on her knees. I could hardly catch my breath. I was dressed in a pretty dress while my twin was wearing short pants and was holding his left hand in his mouth. My hair still has a curl on my forehead just as in the picture. Gienia, my older sister stood in back, while Mother's sister Rozia and her son, Abus, were seated next to her. The two sisters appeared so proud with their beloved, beautiful children.

I stared at this unbelievable find. The photograph was in excellent condition except for a small wrinkle on my sister's face. The reality of putting faces to my ghostly memories made me shiver with joy and a feeling of belonging to real people, while at the same time, evoked feelings of distress and loss. This picture was the greatest treasure beyond my wildest dreams.

When Father's friend from Poland gave us a picture of his twin children, I took possession of the snapshot and carried it around in

Abus, Aunt Rozia, Gienia, Mother Ester and the twins, Ida and Adam

my wallet, thinking that this scene would also have been of my twin and me. Now I finally had the real picture—an image of my mother, sister, and twin, which reawakened and identified my longing for him. I immediately asked Zvi to make copies of this treasure and placed the negative in a bank safe. I sent one of the photos to Father, but he didn't dare to frame nor display it on his wall fearing that Cyvia would not approve.

Zosia explained how she found her mother's old aunt, who she visited often. The aunt's photo album also revealed a picture of my maternal grandparents, but Zosia would not part with that photo, nor trust anyone, even a photographer, to make copies. I finally inherited the picture after Zosia died.

Shortly after we arrived in Chicago, my mother's other sister Roma came to greet us at Zosia's apartment. She arrived leading a three-year-old girl. Roma looked youthful and fashionable, dressed in lacy shorts and a matching halter top. Her hair was the color of a carrot, cut short and swept up toward her face ending on her forehead.

Aunt Zosia remarked as I inspected Aunt Roma, "Don't you have good looking aunts?"

She greeted me with a bright smile and a dancing step. The little girl was introduced as her daughter Aviva. She was the same age as Ester, with blonde, stringy hair and a delicate, almost translucent complexion. She was more petite and sicklier looking. It was surprising that Aunt Roma was allowed to adopt such a young child, when she herself was past middle age. The child was spoiled and had very few social skills with adults or children.

Aunt Roma took us in her new Cadillac to her home in Lincolnwood. The impressive, large home was full of furniture that reminded me of Louis XIV era as seen in museums, and was referred to in modern times as *nouveau riche* (new rich). This was the first house I had ever seen with a basement that was also used as a living room. Every room had huge arrangements of flowers. Aunt Zosia pointed out with a giggle that Aunt Roma told everyone that it was from a secret admirer, but in fact she got them from her gardener who also was the care-taker of a cemetery. Both aunts spoke English until I became fluent. They then switched to Polish, probably not wanting to show that their English was not so good.

Misfortune struck Aunt Roma and Uncle Joe because their little Aviva was killed behind the laundromat, when she was playing inside a carton, and was hit by a car that was parking in the back of the building. Their grief and loss were unimaginable. I held on to my Ester even more carefully and tenderly after this incident.

About a year later, they adopted an infant boy they named David. That child also gave them distress when at the tender age of three, he was diagnosed with kidney cancer. My Uncle Joe, who loved his son very much, must have prayed very hard, because David overcame the cancer and led a normal life from then on.

Right from the beginning of our arrival, I attended free English lessons at the local library in the daytime and at a temple on Pratt Avenue in the evening. Later, I enrolled in a private school downtown, where I learned to use IBM computers. I lacked typing skills, so I bought a used typewriter and taught myself, from a manual, to type the touch system.

I even got my first job in the bookkeeping office at "Queen's Way to Fashion" as a supervisor of the key punch department. In the next few years, I had a lot of working experience in the constantly growing field of computers.

In all those years, Zvi and I did not have a happy marriage, and for a long time, I wanted a divorce. The problems multiplied with the years, and I found it almost intolerable. What held me in the marriage was our daughter. He was controlling and tried to hold me back from developing and striving to reach my potential. He was intolerant when I read books. He did not see the value of adapting to the ways of America.

I was the one who initiated anything new to improve our lives, even learning to drive. He talked a lot about opening a photo studio, like in Netanya, but all it amounted to was words. His lack of looking at how to better our lives disappointed me and fell short of my expectation to provide a better life for our child.

I needed to make sure that our child would have opportunities in this wonderful country and decided that I had to be the one to provide. I opened my own dry cleaning and alteration business on Morse Avenue, by the Morse "L" station. Many customers became good friends. Even though my days and nights were busy with the cleaning store and alterations, I still had all the house chores completed and had no help from Zvi. He only appeared at the store after work to count the money that I had earned daily.

My responsibility and love for Ester held me to continue in this life. She was a charming child and a good student. A bus dropped Ester off from Hebrew school at the store where I always had a cooked meal waiting for her in the back of the store. I had a little television for her and made sure she did her homework before closing the store at seven in the evening. My work continued at home.

Besides the running the household, every evening I brought home a bag filled with alterations that needed to be finished for the following day or two. I was overworked and angry. I thought that I could not endure such a life much longer. But Ester kept me in this difficult marriage.

Again, I went to see the same lawyer that I had consulted seven years earlier but gave up when a flu knocked me off my feet, helpless in bed. I thought about my little daughter who still needed so much care and wondered how would I manage. Now, after all the years of struggling and being overwhelmed by all the responsibilities, I decided it was time to part from my marriage to Zvi. I had realized from the days in Netanya that it was not a marriage. But what choice did I have? Not having a father or mother who would protect me led me to a chain of unfortunate decisions in my life.

When I looked back at my life, I realized that every time I listened to my own inner voice or instincts, I made better decisions than when my father and aunts told me what was good for me. In my early years, I was convinced that the elders knew more, but this did not work for me anymore, especially when the older folks were themselves unstable and even confessed to me that their own lives were failures.

Finally, when Ester was thirteen, going on thirty, I told her about my decision. I was surprised and pleased that she understood. This was the right time for me to finalize my resolve to dissolve the marriage.

The lawyer told me at that meeting, " I think that this time you are really ready."

My divorce was final in 1972, and within three months, I was free to make my own decisions and mistakes. I decided to take matters into my own hands and looked forward to my life ahead of me. I felt sure, and knew, that life would be better. All my difficulties and experiences made me become more mature. I started to believe in my own judgment and inner strength.

I sold the cleaning store and got a new job as a key punch operator, as I had before. From the assets of the store, I purchased a small townhouse in Skokie. Ester was starting her freshman year of high school at Maine East. The transition in her life was a great worry for me, but amazingly, and quickly, she made many new friends, which she kept until the end of high school and beyond. Elizabeth Surlin was and still is her most cherished friend today. I bought Ester a birthday present, a small poodle puppy that we named Pepe. It was a choice between a new carpet or a dog. The dog became a part of our family.

I made friends with single and divorced women, and soon I met an old friend, also a Holocaust survivor, with a similar life experience. As luck would have it, he was the person I was waiting for. He was young at heart, but at the same time mature. I started to feel a strong attraction towards him and realized that this time it was the real thing. We took our time to get to know each other and made sure that there was no pressure to get married. Eventually we did, and I felt that my daughter would be comfortable with my decision.

Sam, a quiet, assured man, treated me with respect and affection, which made me feel confident that marrying him was the right decision. We both felt a great relief that we found each other. I finally was happy and at peace.

Sadly, I learned that Father was suffering from lung cancer, due in part to his many years of heavy smoking. When I realized that Father was not going to recover, I flew to Israel to spend some time with him. At that point he had been fighting cancer for two years and had undergone two operations to remove a section of his lungs in attempt to prolong his life.

When I saw him in October of 1975, he expressed great satisfaction and happiness that I came. He asked many questions about Ester, his only grandchild. At that time, I told him that I planned to marry a wonderful, stable man. He was glad for me and gave me his gold initialed ring and his wedding band. Later I discovered that the inscription inside was my parents' wedding date. He also gave me a silver serving dish, while Cyvia cringed and bit her nails, but she didn't dare to say anything against his decision. She even added that when I returned, she would give me all the silver items they had and a huge crystal punch bowl set we brought from Poland. I came many times after Father's death, and saw Cyvia, but she never gave those things to me. She never intended to give me anything. Later, I found out that she made Father sign off everything to her.

The most unforgivable situation that developed between Cyvia and me was when she neglected to notify me that Father passed away. When I confronted her over the phone, she only answered, "You couldn't change anything anyway!"

What she really was concerned about was that I would fight Father's will, which could be contested for thirty days after a person's passing, as per Israeli law.

I felt abandoned again by my father even in death. My sorrow and loss was now translated into a double loss of not being at Mother's funeral and now Father's. Cyvia, in the meantime, sold all his jewelry and clothing—not even leaving a souvenir for me.

As much as I wanted to resolve all kinds of unfinished business on my last visit, I did not foresee another subject that would disturb my peace after his death. I learned then that Father was married and had a son before he married my mother, which was a deep, dark secret that Aunt Zosia revealed.

The events of his first marriage were hard to hear and understand. It appears that he was a seventeen-year-old boy and worked as a tailor's apprentice for an older widow. Although she was twice his age, she fell in love with him and got pregnant by him. Father felt that the only honorable thing to do was to marry the women for the sake of his child. But the marriage did not last long because his wife got sick and died. So, when Father married Mother, he apparently had the boy with him. Aunt Zosia thought that the boy's name was Emanuel but was not sure. As a toddler, I have no memories of this child and yet, occasionally, veiled scenes pop up with a game or a giggle or tears.

Uncle Joe confirmed that he remembered a young boy in our house while he courted Aunt Roma. No one knows what fate befell Emanuel and my older sister Gienia during the Holocaust. I always think and hope that perhaps they are alive somewhere. After all, I survived.

It was disturbing that the secret was kept till Father's death. I would have wished to know about my half-brother and really get to know Father. But his generation kept such a secret, because for some strange reason it was an embarrassment. Father also must have approved to keep this out of public knowledge, because hc was overly concerned with appearances and what people would say.

23

JOZEFA COMES FOR A VISIT

Sam and I were married in 1976. A few months later, he suggested that I bring my Polish mother for a visit to the USA. I was so overwhelmed and grateful by his offer. It had been my greatest wish, and now Sam was suggesting the very same thing, as if he read my mind.

I immediately wrote to Jozefa to prepare a passport and all legal papers for her to come to see us in Skokie the next summer. I also gave her a choice to keep the airfare money or to come here.

Her answer was, "I am coming."

She wrote about how her neighbor who had mocked her in the past when she spoke about visiting me reacted with disbelief. She would say to her, "I first will see hair growing on the palm of my hand."

We lived in a small townhouse on Kilpatrick Street in Skokie. I fixed up one of the bedrooms just for her with every comfort that I could think of and afford. My family and friends were most supportive and excited about this visit. They and my neighbors all knew that my Polish mother saved me during the Holocaust. All were eager to welcome and meet my hero and rescuer.

LOT, the Polish airline, was the only one flying to Chicago. Its arrival was always a mystery. The Communists created all sorts of obstacles and made life miserable for their citizens and relatives abroad. But my friend Kathy got a hold of the international aviation company and was given the time of arrival for the afternoon. I could hardly work that day. Sam, Ester, and Kathy were coming with me to greet my mother at O'Hare International terminal.

From the second floor, we could observe the passengers going through customs. Other passengers' relatives and friends came to greet the arriving travelers from Poland, holding bouquets of fresh flowers. As we were peering down to the customs area trying to find Josefa, we could discern who were the Polish passengers because they were carrying pillows, probably ill advised that in the USA we have no real goose down. The customs officers were smiling every time they opened up luggage and found bottles of Polish vodka.

Ester was impatiently asking for a description every time she spotted an elderly woman with a cane. I had to correct her that although she was her grandmother, she did not look like the stereotype from the movies with a babushka on her head or walking with a cane. I spotted Josefa, even though it was nineteen years since we had seen each other.

She was wearing a navy blue knit suit, still slim, and her straight gray hair was pinned behind her ears.

We rushed to the customs exit to greet her. As she came out, she was frozen, not knowing what to expect. I grabbed her in my arms and couldn't let go until we both sobbed emotionally. With exhilaration and disbelief, we were embracing each other. Everyone hugged her and tried to express their happiness. All were in awe knowing the great sacrifice she made for a strange Jewish child, who she loved and protected as her own.

Her amazement of experiencing our way of life was like a child discovering a toy store. Every time I took her to the supermarket, she shook her head and exclaimed, "This one store could feed the whole Polish population."

The large, well-stocked, adorned department stores at Old Orchard Mall made her comment, "I feel like I'm walking in a dream. How will I ever be able to explain this at home?"

At Marshall Field's department store, she enjoyed looking around the toy department and bought me a doll. It was to make up for my childhood without toys. From Poland, she brought me two figurines, a boy and a girl doll, dressed in regional Krakow outfits. I told her that to me they represented my missing brother Adam and me. She agreed with a sad smile.

I asked her if she remembers the Christmas Eve I was brought to her by her husband Wilhelm. She answered, "Very well. And a few days

Jozefa Maj, my Polish mother

later I sent him to the Sosnowiec Ghetto to get your twin brother and sister Gienia, but it was too late. He did his best to look for them."

In the evening, when I returned home from work, we walked around parks and shopping malls holding hands. One day I asked Jozefa what ever happened to her own mother whom I vaguely remembered. She told me the tragic story. Her mother committed suicide because she couldn't stand to watch Jozefa being abused by Grandfather Maj when we lived in his apartment. It did not surprise me, but it saddened me.

During the day Mother's best companion was our poodle Pepe, whom she overfed. She loved animals and fed them constantly with the leftovers from our meals. The neighbors complained about stray cats and squirrels coming to our front yard, but there was no stopping her from feeding the world.

When Ester came home from school, she would communicate with Mother Josefa using a Polish-English dictionary. She tried to explain our favorite soap opera, "All My Children." When I returned home from work, I was surprised to find that Mother was able to tell all the details of that day's events on the show. During her visit, Ester learned more Polish than Mother Jozefa English.

To give her more pleasure, I got her a new wardrobe, and every weekend we traveled to different parts of Illinois. Her favorite restaurant was The Barn in Gurnee. We became so close that we were able to discuss our feelings about every subject we could think of. We even promised that whoever died first, we would somehow let the other know that there is a beyond, and we would communicate in times of great need.

When her visit was coming to an end, I asked her if she wouldn't stay with us rather than go back to Poland. With tears in her eyes, she told me that it was very tempting, but she couldn't leave her two grandchildren, whom Wilusia neglected because of her addiction to alcohol. She must go back.

Mother received many presents from my friends. I gave her a new look by getting her a perm, a manicure, and dressing her in a pantsuit. It took me a long time to convince her that women look good in slacks. But she was worried about what her neighbors would say.

With a heavy heart, I took her to the airport. The terminal was again full of Polish travelers going home, but this time the luggage was huge, and the hugs and tears were proportioned to their suitcases.

I found a priest whom I asked to take care of my mother during the flight home. That made her feel better. When I returned home, I could hardly stop crying and could not go to her bedroom for weeks. I saw her image everywhere—in the house, the backyard.

24

ESTER ON HER OWN

When Ester graduated from high school, she enrolled in a local college in Chicago. Because of our financial circumstances, I could not afford to send her to a private university away from home like some of her friends did.

Going away was supposed to be an opportunity to study and become mature and independent, but as I observed, there was not much independence in college. Students were supplied with food and lodging, paid for by their parents. They were only independent to do what they chose: work hard and establish a better future, or waste time and money, being irresponsible with no one to look over their shoulder.

Ester attended Northeastern Illinois University, and her consolation gift for not going away was my old Chevy Nova car, which she drove to school. I always encouraged her to study hard and not to worry about household chores. It was important that I assist her as much as I could to help make her life easier so she could devote her time to studying. She graduated from Northeastern and immediately continued on for her Master's degree at Loyola University in downtown Chicago. Within a short time, she graduated and got a job with a government agency. I was so proud of her. I bless God every day for giving me my beloved, special child.

Ester dated many nice boys. One day, her friend Elizabeth, who was the first of their group to get married, introduced her to her husband's good friend, Bruce. He was a handsome fellow with dark

Ester

brown curly hair and dark brown eyes like Ester's. They almost looked like sister and brother. The attraction was instant, especially when they discovered that they had so much in common. Love for the land of Israel was an important common feeling since Bruce had spent one year in Israel studying at the University of Haifa and spoke fluent Hebrew. His parents were most welcoming to Ester and treated her as one of their children.

Bruce and Ester were engaged for four years until they had enough money to settle down. They were married at Temple Beth El on August 22, 1984, with both parents' blessings. Ester and Bruce made an attractive, loving couple. Next to Ester's birth, her marriage was the most important event of my life.

After Ester married, our bustling, noisy house became very quiet. Every day, when I came home from work, I turned on the television just to serve as background noise. I could not stand being alone in the house. A nagging thought was constantly invading my mind. Why did most people have family to lean on and I had so few? I often pictured how nice it would have been to have my sister Gienia and twin brother Adam at the wedding—to be able to visit with me and share my joyful feelings about my daughter's new life. Why did my mother not survive to be with us and enjoy our family's accomplishments and progress? These questions were troubling my being day and night.

What was it all about, having children, raising them to be independent individuals, and then to miss their constant presence? Yet I was proud that Ester had grown into an independent, modern women—the first in our family to get a Master's degree.

Nightmares tortured me. The nightmares were threatening that I was losing my little girl to the German Gestapo. My migraine headaches created a health crisis in my life. Sam had to drive me to the emergency room more often with the most painful headaches and vomiting. Working through the day at my job became a struggle. All I wanted was to go home and rest my head with ice packs.

25

A BAKERY TURNED INTO
A HOLOCAUST MUSEUM

One summer day, while taking a walk near my home, I noticed a gathering of people across the street from my home. This building looked architecturally out of place in this residential area of Skokie. My curiosity took me to the building where a dedication was taking place. I heard a Rabbi speaking the words "Holocaust" and "Holocaust survivors."

The next few days, as I tried to visit the place, the doors were locked. Checking another day, I noticed a little plaque on the door "The Holocaust Memorial Museum." It was a great surprise to me but not strange. Just two years before, April 19, 1978, the world heard of Nazis trying to march in Skokie to enrage the large Jewish population and especially the many Holocaust survivors who lived there.

When I saw a few cars parked in front of the museum, I walked over and rang the bell. The door was opened. I climbed the stairs to find a number of women gathered, all of whom greeted me cheerfully. Erna Gans, Lisa Derman, and Judy Lachman were among the group. I introduced myself as their neighbor.

They told me that as a result of the unsuccessful march of the Nazis, the Holocaust survivors in the area had decided that they would never allow a Nazi demonstration to happen here or anywhere in the United States. Their mission was to educate and prevent future Holocausts. They concluded that the only way to do this was to educate people about the evil history. They stated that the evil past must be made known and people must learn from it.

These few survivors started this project and donated their life savings to buy this unpretentious building. They decided to gather memorabilia and materials to exhibit at the little museum. This was to serve the local schools and residents, so they could personally experience what this evil era did to innocent people. When I learned that they needed help, I immediately volunteered.

The women embraced me and told me, "You are a Godsent person."

I told them how I survived the war. They looked at me with astonishment and exclaimed, "You are a Holocaust survivor too!"

I immediately understood that this was the place where I belonged. This was where my tortured memories and pain could be dedicated to make a difference. I just did not know how and why God put me on this path.

I started to come twice a week to help the secretary, Pearl Karp, with her work. At one point she told me, "Ida you should also belong to a group just formed who meet at the Jewish Community Center in Skokie. They call themselves, "Holocaust Association of Child Survivors."

She said that a young woman Hannah, and a social worker organized this group, and that they were meeting monthly. I immediately called the Jewish Community Center and learned that they were meeting the first Wednesday of each month at seven in the evening. I shared this information with Sam and decided to go and see what it was all about. The first meeting we attended was on March 5, 1986.

We were received with friendship by a core membership of about a dozen people at that time. Everyone introduced themselves with a brief story of how and where they survived. When it came my turn, a tall attractive blonde with no accent wanted to know more details of how I survived. The people embraced us right from the start, as if we had known each other since childhood. Our belonging and purpose were established immediately.

For many meetings, our members still suffered with flowing tears over their horrific experiences and lost families. It took many meetings to finally understand our purpose. We pondered what the point of our meetings was and what we were supposed to do with our experiences. And it slowly came out, in a process of discussions, agreements, and disagreements, what we were here for.

HACS was a home where we were able to validate our memories of our childhood sufferings. They were real, and we did suffer. We did have something to say and offer to the history of the Holocaust. Child survivors and hidden children are the last witnesses. Many determinations were established, some through witnessing and others by acknowledging that children are also survivors. We confirmed that we were not defeated. Through our searching, sharing our survival stories with students and adult groups, and attending conferences, we learned that many Holocaust survivors established successful lives in many fields.

When we began to share our experiences with young and adult audiences, we were admired for overcoming all odds and becoming regular, useful people, not damaged in spirit. We blended into every society in every country in which we lived. Many of us became renowned professionals, doctors, lawyers, artists, and writers. And, in almost every arena, we were outstanding assets to society, and we did it on our own. There were no support groups, no psychologists to counsel us about our personal losses and the childhood that turned us immediately into adults.

In time, we had discovered that in other cities throughout the United States and later the world, child survivors were finding each other and embracing one another with a joy that is hard to describe. We found that our life survival stories and legacy must be preserved and passed on, to educate the world, so people will understand what anti-Semitism, racism, and hate brings about.

Forty years after the Holocaust, we started to come out of hiding, or rather finally people started to listen to our lives. Many books were being published and shared in schools and libraries.

The Holocaust Memorial Foundation, spurred by the Nazi march, expanded its activity to promote legislation and finally succeeded in having a law passed in Illinois, the first of such laws in the nation, to make it mandatory that the history of the Holocaust be taught in schools. Just a few years later, many Jew haters wanted to abolish the new law. Many deniers of the Holocaust were and are spewing old hate. This cannot be allowed to happen.

The lessons of the Holocaust are not only lessons to prevent such an evil event from happening to Jews, but also to teach and protect all people. We stand against genocide, oppression, discrimination—to protect all people. "Never Again" means "Never Again."

The Holocaust Memorial Foundation, under the leadership of Lisa Derman, established a speakers' bureau, where survivors, child survivors, hidden children, and liberators share their survival experiences in schools and at other venues. I found a purpose.

Through my suffering and sad history, I am able to bring attention to the power that each person has. My hope is that our voices, our lives will matter—will make a difference. Every person has to learn and understand the human tragedy that debases the soul. The lesson of accepting all people and working to create a better world for all is not a choice but a commitment—a life force. Through sharing my story, I am able to show that good people made a difference in my life. I was saved by my Polish family. They saved me to continue my Jewish heritage and my family.

26

CLASS REUNION, TEL-AVIV
DECEMBER 17, 1988

After my visit to Brazil in 1987, my friends and I came up with a plan to hold a class reunion in Tel Aviv. I contacted as many of our Sholom Aleichem School schoolmates and teachers from Wroclaw that I could locate. A lovely hotel was reserved for the reunion.

A problem cropped up when the Israeli security were very cautious and strict to issue visas to citizens from Communist countries, even if they were Jews. I wrote a letter to the Israeli embassy in Berlin, and finally permission was granted.

One of my Sholom Aleichem friends, Roman Zuzowski, lived in Israel and was a general in the Israeli Army. Of course, I was overwhelmed and in awe of what my young friends from Poland had accomplished and their contributions to the safety of Jews.

I wrote to everyone to send me copies of photographs they had from our school. I was creating a yearbook similar to those published in the States. Since I didn't have the budget or know-how, I did it in the least costly and simple way. I worked for accountants at that time and bought folders like they gave their customers. I made copies of all the pictures and made a directory of everyone's information like birth dates, professions, name of spouse, their children, and addresses.

When Sam and I arrived at Israel's airport, Roman was waiting for us, and because of his military rank, he was allowed to welcome us before we went through customs. He did change after all the years, but I recognized him immediately. We arrived early at the hotel glowing with excitement in meeting my classmates that I had not seen since leaving Poland in 1957.

Hotel Carlson, on the beachfront of Tel Aviv, was an inspiring setting for our gathering. The room was large and decorated with flowers. Eighty people, including some spouses of classmates, and three teachers were in attendance. I welcomed everyone as they entered. And as always, my photographic memory did not disappoint me. Soon happy shrieks and sounds of pleasure were heard all over the room, followed by tears, hugs, and kisses.

But before all the festivities started, we handed armfuls of flowers to our teachers, Moshe Brandes, Moshe Cwirn, and Minia Fuks who were overwhelmed by the attention. Mr. Brandes wrote a special poem for that evening that I later translated in prose to English.

Dear Gathered Children - that's you!

I welcome you with all my heart! Heaven sent to me my dearest children, Close to my heart, my gold, my treasure!

And think of that, you children are close to fifty!!!

I remember you when you were small, cheerful, playful and worry free.

But life did not stay still.

The waters on which you swam got stirred again.

And the winds spread you around the world like seeds.

As I gathered from your addresses, you live all over the world.

Today I welcome you with warmest greetings.

I call it our holiday of unification.

I praise you for organizing this reunion. There are no words to describe my feelings.

Praise Ida, Sioma, and all of you who bonded us together again! I send regards to those, who for different reasons did not come.

And I want you to remember those who are dead,

And at last, my wish is to hear from you good news for years to come!

My dearest gathered children from all over the world!

Moshe Brandes — Israel, 12-17-88

I approached the microphone and found myself overwhelmed, feeling my constant longing—something missing. I needed to share my burden of my lost siblings, the shocking death of my mother, my life.

I spoke about the Holocaust, which was our common childhood, but for me it was a silent voice, a yearning, that somewhere my twin, my brother, Adam, was calling me. I could not give up my constant search for my siblings. I could not let go. With sorrow, I was starting to lose hope.

Everyone listened to me with tears in their eyes. The reunion embraced our childhoods with love expressed by all.

27

HERE COME DANIEL AND JONATHAN

In 1988, Ester and Bruce informed us that they were expecting a baby. This news energized and motivated me to excel in my daily activities. Coworkers and friends - whoever would listen - knew about my exciting news.

On December 4, 1989, Daniel Adam was born. My love overwhelmed me for this innocent little being, my grandchild. I was amazed that this kind of love could happen so instantly. My joy was beyond description.

"What a pretty baby," was heard as people looked at this cherub with blonde hair, blue eyes, and long, dark lashes. I was overjoyed to be with Daniel and danced around the house cradling him in my arms every chance I got. I talked to him explaining his surroundings and creating stories of every picture on the wall. My life seemed complete, and I found some peace with Daniel's arrival.

A couple of weeks after Daniel's arrival, on December 16, 1989, I could not find enough people to express my feelings to and was driven to write the following letter to my grandson.

"Daniel's arrival fills a void that I felt after Esti married Bruce and left the nest. Now I know that every day I have to look forward to a magic brought with his being. I have feelings that I longed for a long time since Ester's birth. I don't know how to express them, but I know that there is room to fill the empty space with a new kind of love that I could not imagine.

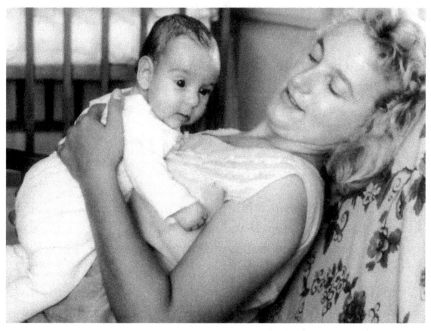

Ida mother of Ester

As I look at Daniel, I know that he needs to be protected from what I lived through. It is not because his parents don't give him enough love, but my experiences cry out that my grandchild deserves more. He is blessed to have grandparents that Ester and I did not have because the Holocaust robbed us from the love of our dear ones.

I looked at Daniel for hours and constantly wished that I wouldn't have to go to work and miss his daily new developments. But perhaps it is better that I worked so that my dear Ester would have the opportunity of cuddling with her lovely little boy alone. I am ready and will be there for my treasure Daniel when he or his parents need me."

My second grandson was born on October 5, 1994. Jonathan weighed almost ten pounds and looked very much like his mother when she was born. The first letter "J" of his name was to remember my Polish mother Jozefa.

28

REAWAKENED SEARCH

A woman from the Red Cross, who visited the Skokie Holocaust Museum, gave us a report that after the fall of the Soviet Union, old secret documents were being opened to the public, including thousands that were captured by the Soviet Army. Currently, they were being transferred to the United States and other countries. She informed us that now we could apply again to the Red Cross to renew searches of missing families.

Many people did, and I encouraged our small Holocaust Association of Child Survivors group to fill out forms and mail them to the Red Cross. It took two years before they informed me that due to overwhelming inquiries, they couldn't handle all the cases and advised me to do it myself. I was given a few locations to write. I followed the advice and started searching for my siblings, in earnest, through these sources.

My search extended everywhere I could think of, including the United States. I wrote to the Social Security Administration offices to see if Adam or Gienia Paluch were possibly registered with them, but the answer was negative. I then wrote to an agency in Israel who had success in finding lost relatives, but the answer from them was also negative.

In 1991, the first conference of Hidden Children was held at the Marriott Hotel in New York City. They expected about two hundred survivors, but in fact an overwhelming response of more than 2,000 people arrived. No reports in the newspaper or on television could adequately describe the atmosphere of that gathering. Unexpectedly, people were finding old friends and relatives that they never dreamed of meeting again.

Three floors of the giant hotel were taken over by the Hidden Child Survivors. In the middle level, there were bulletin boards displaying an overwhelming number of announcements, notes, and pictures. Feverishly, everyone searched for a familiar face. I, too, posted photocopies of pictures of my mother, father, sister (who was about seven in my picture), and my twin brother, Adam, and I sitting on Mother's lap. I pinned a note under the picture with a request, *"If anyone knows the whereabouts of these children, please leave a message."*

I checked back many times during the two days, but there were no replies. But there was a clue of another possibility. A small group of child survivors had come as delegates from Poland, and some had recently discovered that they were Jews. They had been hidden and adopted into families - not always officially - and learned the truth about their identities only at the deathbeds of their adoptive parents.

My friends Halina Masri and Stephanie Seltzer were also drawn to speak to the Polish group. At one point, we had a workshop together, and each of us told about ourselves. It immediately reinforced my hope that maybe my siblings survived like I did. I thought of going to Poland and meeting every one of those Polish survivors myself.

Towards the end of the conference, to my great surprise, I discovered a photo of a group of children with my husband Sam's face looking at me. The note accompanying the picture asked to contact a telephone number, which I copied, and then I immediately called Sam to tell him of this find. When I returned home, we called the number ,and as it turned out, it was a girl from my husband's orphanage in France from after the war. Sam and Vera were happily reunited, and that same summer, we went to Florida to visit them.

At the annual gathering of Holocaust Child Survivors in Alexandria, Virginia, one of the attractions was a visit to the newly built Holocaust Museum in Washington D.C. A special focus was the exhibit called *Remember the Children*. I had seen part of the exhibit when it was brought to the Museum of History in Chicago. Many of our local survivors volunteered as docents. Holocaust survivors, like myself, were telling visitors about their personal war experiences.

Skipping this exhibit in DC, I went around checking each photograph with a magnifying glass, especially the ones that showed crowds of helpless people guarded by the Gestapo.

On my second visit to the museum with Sam, we were able to spend over a half a day in the upstairs library, looking through the archives of Holocaust survivors and the murdered victims. With hope and determination, I searched for my family name and found another Paluch. With the help of the museum staff, I tried to get in touch with her, but she was not interested in being contacted. Sam's and my name appeared on the list of survivors, and we hoped that someone would try to find us.

About that time, the movie *Shoah*, which was shown at a local high school, captured my attention and affected me greatly. I watched the entire movie for eight hours straight. Every mention of Sosnowiec gave me a clue of a date and what happened to the people of my birth town. It gave me an idea as to when my mother was driven to despair to commit suicide, and when the last transport to a death camp took place. Many questions came to mind, and I was determined to come up with some answers.

There was an inner voice that continually resonated that someone out there was waiting for me to find them. This voice did not give me peace. I decided to go to the Skokie Public Library to learn all I could and got very involved with the history of Jews—my ancestors. The five volumes of the *History of the Jews* by Professor H. Graetz, opened up lessons that I missed when I was in Poland. There were many books that caught my attention during my exploration, but the five volumes were most special to me. I inhaled the material. It was like an addiction to suddenly discover information about my people that had been hidden by the Communists under their occupation of Poland after WW II.

29

AFTER 53 YEARS, I EXPERIENCE
AN EXPLOSION OF EMOTIONS

My endless search was known to all my friends around the world. My friend Lusia Hack, who lived in Connecticut, sent me an article from a local Jewish newspaper. It was about a Holocaust child survivor who was interviewed in Warsaw by a Connecticut reporter. Lusia wrote on the page in Polish that she sent me, *"To jest bardzo ciekawe."* (This is very interesting).

I stared at a photograph of a bearded man, who appeared to be in his fifties. This face looked so familiar. I questioned, *why do I know this face? This face I saw before, where have I seen him?* I peered and even looked with a magnifying glass. *Where have I see him before?*

Suddenly, I was transfixed and could not move or utter a sound. The picture of my Grandfather Moishe, hanging in the hall, was almost a duplicate image of the one in the newspaper. It cannot be, but it can, because there it was, the two faces were almost identical.

*Grandmother Ryvka Wellner Wejntraub and Grandfather Moishe Yidel
Wejntraub*

I read and reread the article with great interest. The article
mentioned the man didn't know his real identity, only that he was
taken by his foster parents from an orphanage. The ribbon bracelet
he was wearing from the orphanage had the name of Tomcio on it.
The man in the paper, whose name was Jerzy Dolebski, was also known
as Tomcio. How could this be? My nickname in school was also *Tomcio
Paluszek*, Tom Thumb, because my last name, Paluch, means thumb.
I froze—my thoughts in turmoil. I left the article on the kitchen
chair and looked at it for days. I mentioned to my husband that it
could be my twin brother, Adam. I was wrestling with myself,
wondering what to do. Was it possible that after fifty- three years, I
was about to discover my lost twin, Adam? It became a constant
question. Every day I became more certain.

The picture of my grandparents seemed to be speaking to me. It
would not let me rest. Such a miracle does not happen to me. My life
has been a struggle, living with ghostly memories of running after

Mother with my twin and sister chasing after her. These were my last shocking memories of losing my mother and my siblings.

Earlier, an extraordinary event happened. A bird flew into our house, and I was sure that the bird was a messenger. One night, during this time of debating with myself about what should I do, an unusual sound woke me from a restless sleep. I heard a loud noise at our front door. I got up to check what it was and found that the Polish figurines of the boy and girl in national Krakow costume, were on the floor, broken. They were the figurines Mother Jozefa had given me when she visited us in Skokie. She told me then that they represented my brother and me.

How they wound up on the floor was a mystery. I looked at the mess and actually said out loud that the broken figurines must be a message from Mother. When she was here, we talked a lot about God, death, and meeting each other in the afterlife. I asked her, jokingly, if she would send me a sign from the other side. With an earnest, intense look, she promised that she would. Mother Jozefa passed away in 1980. I was not able to go to her funeral, but I prayed for her.

That evening, I decided to take action. I had to find the Connecticut reporter, Deborah Kazis. I called Stephanie Seltzer, who knew people involved in Holocaust causes all over the United States. Within a week, on January 13, 1995, I got a call from the young lady who interviewed Jerzy Dolebski in Warsaw. I told her about my suspicions and asked her if the man had any memories of his childhood. She told me that he didn't remember a thing. I realized that this is why no one could find him. I asked her for Jerzy Dolebski's contact information. She had his address but not his phone number. She suggested that I inquire at the office of the Jewish Joint Organization in Krakow. She gave me the office number. On my lunch break, I called the office and eventually received a message on my answering machine that they knew Jerzy Dolebski and left me his home phone number.

I called immediately, and my first words were, "May I speak to Jerzy Dolebski?"

A young man's voice answered that Mr. Dolebski was not home but that he was his son and would take a message.

Hurriedly I blurted out, "I think that your father is my twin brother. Please tell him to call me collect any time, even during the night."

The son called his mother to the phone who was not too surprised by the news. She promised that the minute her husband returned from Warsaw, she would give him this message. That evening, the phone rang. I jumped to answer because I knew it was him. The operator asked if I would accept a collect call from Jerzy Dolebski, and I screamed "Yes!"

A polite voice told me how hard it was to get through because my message said I lived in Chicago, but I lived in Skokie, a suburb of Chicago. It had a different area code. He asked me to hang up the phone so he could call me from his telephone at his own expense. Before I had time to object, he hung up.

It seemed like an eternity, but a minute later the phone rang again. My heart was pounding, and I felt giddy and faint. The first thing he asked me was why did I believe that he was my twin brother. I told him about the article of his interview in Warsaw and his picture that looked like our grandfather.

The next questions he asked were, "How old are you? When were you born?"

I answered that we were born May 3, 1939.

He answered, "I don't think I am your twin brother because I was born on October 15, 1942."

I asked him if he was sure. He answered yes and that his Christian birth certificate says so.

"So does mine," I answered. "My Christian birth certificate says that I was born in 1942, but I know for sure that it isn't true because my father found me and told me when and where I was born."

Jerzy Dolebski was not fully convinced and suggested that if I would come to Poland, he would help me look for my brother. I was very disappointed and helpless. Before I made the phone call, I was worried that if I gave him too much information, he would try to match his biography to mine. There are many people in the world who would be glad to pretend to be a relative just to come to the United States. But this man did not care.

I asked him if he would mind sending me a picture of himself at the youngest age he has and a picture without a beard. He promised he would. He also told me that I could send him any mail by fax on the same telephone number.

Thoughts of doubt crept in. I was frustrated because I felt that I did not prove to Jerzy that he was my twin. Was I fooling myself—wanting desperately for him to be my brother? I decided to continue my quest and see if anything matched. I made copies of photographs I had and wrote a description of everyone in the photo.

Adam and his foster mother

In ten days, I got a letter from Jerzy with a bunch of photographs. As I looked at them, his face was so familiar to me. In one of the pictures he sent, from the youngest age, he is holding the hand of his foster mother dressed in an overcoat and a hat. The round face with light hair looked the way my twin looked on Mother's lap in the picture was from 1944. He was about five-years old, but his height seemed more like three. I, too, was always small for my age because of the poor nourishment during the war.

Another picture showed when he was a teenager. Here I saw a very strong resemblance. The only difference was that Adam became dark like our father, and I was still light like our mother.

Ida and Adam

The most shocking and scary information was that he had no memory from before 1944. But in the letter, he mentioned that he remembered one prayer, "God help Mommy and Daddy, and *Panie Leonie.*" Mr. Leon in English. I screamed out loud, repeating this sentence. I immediately called Jerzy. Now I knew for sure that he was my brother. I asked him, "Do you want to repeat your childhood prayer to me again?" He did. I asked him if he was aware of the name Mr. Leonie. He said no. I told him, "You were praying for your father, his name was Leon. And the picture you have sent me of your oldest son is an exact image of Father."

Adam, that is what I must call him, told me that when he got my faxed pictures, his middle son immediately showed him his own picture when he was age two. He pointed at me in the picture   and said, "Look Father, this child on the woman's lap looks like me."

And indeed, he does. The only thing is that everyone mixes us up. They point to me in the picture saying, this must be the boy, and then they point to Adam and say this is the girl. The resemblance of our parents was obviously very visible in Adam's children. His youngest son looks like my daughter Ester, even as baby.

This is the first time Adam learned his true name, Adam Paluch. He even recollects that his foster father Mr. Dolebski called him by his nickname, *"Tomcio Paluszek"* because he knew his real name and didn't want to disclose it to Adam.

I had no more doubt. I was convinced that I found my twin brother. He, too, accepted me as his sister. We cried on the phone. From that time, we had a great need to see each other. A great longing overcame me, and I promised Adam that the moment the income tax season was over where I worked, I would come to Poland. We started to miss each other, and it became very painful to wait.

I still cannot explain why I did not go to Poland immediately. I really don't have an answer. Maybe I needed time to recover from the shock of discovery that after fifty-three years, since the tragic day when we witnessed our Mother's death, my twin brother survived.

I was sobbing every day just thinking how far Adam was from me. And in a strange way he got my message, for whenever I felt most desperate to talk to him, he would call. I realized how lucky we were that we did not end up in Auschwitz.

We called each other every week, then every few days, then twice a day. This phone calling became a source of worry for our families. They saw our compulsion of needing to connect often. To them, it seemed that it was over the top. For me, it was a magnetic pull of my connection to my twin, as is proven in science that such a bond is beyond understanding.

At that time, many people, including my daughter,, Ester and cousin Guta wanted to come to Poland with me. But I wanted no distractions when I met my brother. I needed to be able to spend every minute with Adam and discover anything and everything about our lives and the past. Our lives were uprooted. We survived every kind of suffering and abandonment.

It was established that I would come to Warsaw on April 28, 1995. Finally, the day of my departure came. In the preceding weeks, I shopped for gifts for Adam and his family. Our birthday was coming up on May 3, and this would be the first time, after fifty-three years, that we would celebrate together. What should I buy that would be meaningful for his birthday? It didn't take long to come up with the right gift. My first and last choice was a *mezuzah* to wear around his neck, so it would always be close to his heart.

I bought shirts, sweaters, Bulls basketball team caps, even underwear and socks for his sons. I remembered Mother Jozefa mentioned that her grandsons were in need of those hard-to-get articles of clothing. For Adam's wife, whatever I bought for myself, I bought for her, including cosmetics.

Ready to go, I got an easy travel pantsuit, a trench coat, and a bright fashionable scarf. I wanted my brother to be pleased with how I looked. I wanted the first impressions to be of a modern woman.

Sam drove me to O'Hare Airport, questioning if I was doing the right thing. I did not answer him. He knew what my answer would be. I found LOT Airlines and the gate listed on the monitor. I knew that I was at the right place when I heard people speaking Polish, some holding flowers. The custom of greeting or saying goodbye with flowers was evident here and was welcoming.

Sam again said in a nervous voice, "Maybe I should come with you."

I assured him that I would be okay and not to worry. After all, this was not the first time I was traveling to Poland by myself. I promised to call and tell him about my meeting and first impressions of Adam and his family.

I tried to stay calm and to put aside my worrisome thoughts and expectations. Thankfully, exhausted from all the months of apprehension of what and who would meet me, I fell asleep. The next thing, I awoke and saw that we were flying low for a landing.

Checking the passport went fast, but finding my suitcase was another story. The long wait to get my luggage made me worry that the suitcase was lost. I had this experience when I visited Poland during the Communist times in 1980. My anxiety grew. I was anxious to meet Adam. I was preoccupied worrying about the luggage when it finally appeared— it was last on the conveyor. Wheeling my luggage, I proceeded through customs where they thankfully did not bother me with any searches or questions.

As I stepped out through the doors from customs, I noticed a large crowd waiting for passengers. At the end of the waiting hall, I noticed a bearded man with an anxious face and eyes that locked into mine like magnets. I was transfixed and knew instantly that here stood my brother.

We ran into each other's arms, as blinding flashes of cameras and spotlights zeroed in on us. I heard a great gasp of relief from   the crowd as we hung onto each other.

I was not paying attention to anything around me. I was overwhelmed with a joy, instant love, and satisfaction that I found him—I was now with Adam. We were together. It felt like a great weight was lifted from my heart. I was released from my years of searching. All I could do was thank God for this unbelievable miracle of our survival and reunion.

As we held each other, I heard Adam's voice telling me, "I am going to faint. Take me to a seat."

Slowly I led him to a chair, and immediately we found ourselves surrounded by people poking microphones in my face, asking questions.

With breathless words, all I could say, "This is my brother!"

Adam and I were trembling and crying. We could not stop looking at each other in disbelief, fearing that this was not real and that it was a dream that might disappear. I looked into his eyes and saw green eyes looking back at me. The family told me that my eyes were like Mother's. We held each other's hands and continued staring at each other with awe and pain.

Adam pointed to a young man with dark hair and dark eyes standing nearby, "This is my youngest son."

I reached out to greet him, but he backed away from my touch. Adam then introduced two women; both were blonde and about our age. Guta, a child survivor from Canada, who came to attend the Holocaust Child Survivors' gathering to be held in the city of Zakopane in May, and the other Bieta Ficowska, also a child survivor, who referred to herself as a sister to Adam.

Bieta asked me, "Are you sure that Adam is your brother now that you see him?"

My answer was emphatic and passionate, "Now more than ever," and I proceeded to open the photo album with pictures of our parents and pictures of Adam's sons, who definitely resembled us as children and as adults.

Guta's face was full of smiles and her eyes full of tears. Bieta's face had a slight cynical smile and a look of disbelief, but she politely asked us to join her in her home for breakfast. I decided not to be affected by her look and spoil one of the most important and happiest days of my life.

Adam's son was taking a video of our reunion. The Israeli TV was also there, along with a crew of reporters from the Gdansk Television station that Adam invited to document this event. They immediately understood the importance of our finding each other and decided to follow us for the next few days. Adam invited the producers, Mr. and Mrs. Kalukin, to our birthday celebration to be held at Adam's home.

As we drove from the airport, we were absorbed only in each other. We were talking and asking questions and did not notice a police car following us. He stopped us after a few miles.

A young officer came to the passenger side and asked with a stern voice, "Are you aware that you were speeding?"

I implored in a pleading voice, "Please don't spoil our happiest day. We just met after a fifty-three -year separation."

He looked dubiously at us and stated, "But you don't look old enough to be separated for fifty-three years."

I showed him my American passport and Adam, his driver's license. He looked us over and spotted my suitcase and the roses that Adam greeted me with. He was finally convinced and said in an emotional voice, "I don't want to be the cause of spoiling your most unusual day, so congratulations and drive with care." We thanked him and continued on our way.

Adam drove to Bieta's, where we met her husband, a popular published Polish writer and poet. He had an interesting face and appeared much older than his wife. His large blue eyes and bald head reminded me of a space character from a science fiction movie. He welcomed us with a friendly, warm attitude and spent some time speaking with us, which according to my brother, was a rare occurrence.

After a short visit, we proceeded on our journey to my home city, Wroclaw where we were invited to a wedding by my friend Teresa Wozniak. She and I had become close friends when she was in Chicago. Our friendship continued even after she returned to Poland and again during her next visit to the States. Her second trip was sponsored by my invitation to work. She was loyal and helpful to Mother Jozcfa. The two of them became dear friends. When I came to Poland in 1980, and then returned with Sam in 1990, we were welcome guests of Teresa and her family.

Lidia Policinska, from Czestochowa, was another friend that lived in Jozefa's building and was a great help to Mother. She was a teacher to Jozefa's grandsons, Artur and Adam. When Jozefa returned from her visit with me in Skokie, she bragged about it to everyone. That is when Lidia approached her to ask me for a tourist invitation. I responded that any friend of my mother's is a friend of mine. They were helpful to Mother, getting whatever she needed for her everyday life.

Adam and I were very tired but exhilarated when we arrived in the late evening to Wroclaw. Teresa welcomed us with excitement and warmth. We hugged and jumped like little children, happy to see each other. The air was charged with the excitement of our arrival and because of the wedding that was taking place the next day.

Teresa put us up in their children's bedroom, but Adam and I spent very little time sleeping. Our conversation went on past midnight. Every time I said goodnight, Adam had another question or topic to discuss. I reminded him about the wedding and that we needed a little sleep. Again, we said goodnight, and in so doing, I started to sing a lullaby which spontaneously both our voices blended with the same tune and words, *"Aaa kotkie dwa, szare bure obydwa."* (Ah ah sleep, two gray- beige kittens.)

As if prompted by some spirit, we turned up the lights and asked each other, "How do you know this lullaby?"

Neither could remember ever singing it before. The lullaby came from somewhere inside our subconscious memories. It must have been a tender time when we were cuddled in our mother's arms.

The next morning, Adam surprised me by shaving off his beard. He immediately looked years younger. He dressed for the wedding in a fashionable, light blue, double-breasted suit with a matching tie and looked as up-to-date as if he shopped in New York. I was pleased to have such an upbeat brother, which brought back visions and images of our fashionable father.

We went to the City Hall, where we met Teresa's son Radek and his bride, the future in-laws, and guests. It was a very exciting ceremony for us. There were other couples waiting to be married. All were dressed beautifully, in contrast to my last visit in 1990, when Poland was under Communist rule.

From City Hall, we were driven to an Army Officer's Club where a reception of breakfast, lunch, and dinner was held. It was a whole day celebration. The musicians were located in an adjoining room, playing without a break, while the guests were served all day, all sorts of food and delicacies.

We were honored by being seated with Teresa and her husband, Andrzej, and the bride's parents, who were a youthful and jovial couple. He was a military physician and that's how he was able to get the huge military club hall for his daughter's wedding. The food that was served was equal to the fanciest hotel in the States.

The elation of the crowd and happy mood also affected Adam and me as we joined the dancers. We danced as if we had rehearsed together for years. He definitely had our father's love for music and dancing. As the time passed, I came to see that Adam was very much like Father, appreciating current fashions and striving for the better things in life.

The following day we continued our drive to Wejherowo. Because Adam is a diabetic since his youth, we had to make many stops along the way for him to take catnaps in his car. It was hard to hear that Adam was not in the best of health. He had health issues and problems with his eyesight and other maladies.

It was eerie at times when we expressed the same thoughts at the same time. We chose the same food from menus and wanted to visit the same places. After being taken aback with all these coincidental thoughts and tastes, at one point we decided to write down our thoughts on paper. When we compared what we wrote, with amazement we discovered that had written the same thing.

When we finally arrived at Adam's home, we were greeted by loud barking on the stairway. The door was pushed open by a dog's paws, and a large German shepherd ran toward Adam, holding a slipper in his mouth.

As we entered a large foyer, Adam's wife, an attractive brunette, greeted us with an inquisitive look. His two sons, the middle son and the eldest, startled me as I saw a young version of our father standing in front of me. The elder had an even more striking resemblance to Father than the picture that Adam had sent me. I knew that if ever I would see him on the street anywhere in the world, I would definitely stop and ask him if he was related to the Paluch family. I shared my thoughts with all of them, and it pleased his son and certainly me when I heard him call me Aunt. After the awkward introduction, I opened my suitcase and gave each one a gift that I had brought, which were received with pleasure and friendliness.

Adam's home was spacious with high ceilings. The living room was especially large, even by American standards. The apartment was well-furnished and kept immaculately. The modern luxuries, a large-screen color TV and a video recorder, attainable by few, were enjoyed here by Adam's family. The kitchen was modern and well-equipped. Next to the kitchen, there were two more bedrooms and two full baths. In one they had a small washer and dryer. Adam proudly explained that he, with help from his sons, remodeled the upstairs rooms. I was pleased to see that Adam was able to provide these luxuries and comfort for his family.

The yard next to the building led to a garden with a few fruit trees. About 100 yards in front of the six-flat building was Adam's garage where he kept his car. In addition, Adam owned two stores attached to the right of the building. He collected rent from the tenants. One store was a grocery and the other an ice-cream parlor, also serving beverages.

Wejherowo was a charming small town not far from Gdansk. In the next few days, I met his wife's relatives and Adam's foster family. His wife's sister and her husband came to visit, out of curiosity. I noticed that his wife and her family had dark hair and a darker complexion. Their ancestors came from France. It seemed odd that French people would want to come and live in Poland with its harsh climate and a less metropolitan life. I suspected that they had Jewish ancestors; Adam had the same thoughts. My speculations were in a way confirmed by his wife's sister when she told me that one day, when they arrived in their Cadillac at a cinema, some teenagers proclaimed aloud, "This is how a Jewess looks."

Adam proudly introduced me to everyone he knew in his town. Walking together and holding hands became a habit for us. Soon his wife was overcome with jealousy of our close bond and demanded that Adam not display hand holding in public. Her unfounded mistrust brought about inquiry of our sleeping arrangements when we traveled and stayed overnight on the various trips we took. I was offended and hurt by her suspicions and insinuations.

I felt free trusting Adam. He was my brother. My growing love for him was strictly as my brother. Questioning our sleeping arrangements was insulting. I did not take notice to these insinuations and did not discuss it.

Adam took me to his doctor, Dr. Loss-Fiszor, to get his sugar reading—he could not afford to have this instrument at home. His doctor took me aside, away from Adam, and told me that in the death camp Majdanek, Adam was used for medical experiments. He was not in good health, and he needed better treatment. His well-being depended on good healthcare.

When we went to Warsaw to meet the child survivors and the staff of the Tomaszewski Synagogue, we came across people who expressed happiness for our finding each other. Many cried when Adam introduced me as his lost twin sister after fifty-three years. There were some who doubted and questioned that something like our reunion could possibly be true after so many years. I, too, could not believe it, but I recognized our miracle and had to pinch myself every day to make sure it wasn't a dream.

The Gdansk TV producers invited themselves to videotape us at our birthday party. Guta, who was at the Warsaw airport to greet us, attended our birthday celebration. That was the day that I met Adam's foster family who didn't recognize Adam without the beard.

They tried to be receptive but were tentative to accept this miracle. Finally, they did accept, understanding his life-long search to find his own roots and family. The air was filled with tension.

When Adam introduced me to his foster father, he said, "This is my sister, Ida."

The father reacted apprehensively and could not repeat my name. To mask his agitation, he uttered, "If this is your sister, that means she is my daughter. Now I have three daughters."

His wife stated with disbelief, "Who could believe that such an event could happen, and so much time passed since you saw each other?"

Adam proclaimed, "I pray that we should never see the day that we should be separated again."

I replied, "With God's help we will always be together."

The TV crew was videotaping everything and everyone siting around the table. Then I gave my brother his birthday gift, a golden *mezuzah* and chain.

Adam's foster father, tried to guess what it was, "Is it an airplane?" The Dolebski's eldest son, who came with his wife, also guessed,

"Is it a miniature anvil?"

I explained that it contains a special prayer of blessings and good luck. Also, it symbolized the covenant and the Ten Commandments, which were brought down from Mt. Sinai by Moses and given to the Jewish people. I added that the commandments guide us in our everyday life.

Adam had prepared me not to be shocked by his foster father's anti-Semitic jokes, especially when he had an audience, despite the rumor that he may be of Jewish descent. The rumors were that he was born out of wedlock when his mother worked as a maid for a Jewish family in Hrubieszow.

The more I listened to this man, the harder it was to believe that he was really a man of good intentions and deeds. He was credited with saving Adam during the war. Yet I could not believe what I was hearing and questioned how he could be so unfeeling and prejudiced. Soon I discovered that he was not the one who saved my brother.

Adam told me that he wanted to honor his parents as Righteous Among Nations. He submitted their names to Yad Vashem, the Holocaust Memorial and Museum in Jerusalem. They documented selfless saviors by planting a tree, in their name, on the Avenue of the Righteous in Jerusalem.

When Adam finally brought his foster parents to Warsaw to be interviewed by the representative of Yad Vashem, it appeared that they didn't save him during the Holocaust, but in actuality, took him from an orphanage in Lublin when he was just five years old in 1944, days after the liberation. The orphanage was located near the infamous concentration camp Majdanek.

Adam's foster parents calculatingly took a Jewish child and were paid for his upkeep by the orphanage. The overcrowded conditions forced the orphanage to let Polish people take children and care for them. It was also expected that anyone who had Jewish children would return them to the Jewish community.

During the Yad Vashem interview, Adam finally learned about some of their secrets, which were previously concealed from him. They even deliberately misled him in his search for his identity and family. All kinds of stories were told to him about how he was found by the Dolebskis and adopted. They claimed they found Adam in an orphanage but could not remember where.

They told him another story that before the war, they knew many Jews in Hrubieszow. A woman named Frida Noymark, who was single and had a child out of wedlock, gave them her child to save from death. When Adam started to trace this lead, he found out that there was a woman with this name, but she never had a child. There were many versions, but none could be traced. Adam even traveled to Israel to look for people who might recognize him. He was written up in Israeli newspapers, while the Orthodox community tried to help him, without success.

After this pilgrimage to Israel, he became very depressed but still did not give up on his lifelong search. His search started at the young age of eight or nine. He, on his own, went to Warsaw to the Jewish community where they questioned him about any memories, names of his birth parents, and where he was born, but the only answer he got is that he may be a disturbed child.

Finally, a break came when he joined the Holocaust Child Survivors in Poland who were organized after the 1991 gathering of Hidden Children in New York. He joined this small group of 150 survivors, which grew in number to many hundreds.

While he was attending a gathering, he was singled out for an interview by an American reporter, Deborah Kazis. She was visiting Warsaw to learn about the Holocaust Child Survivors in Poland. Her article was published in a Connecticut Jewish paper "The New Haven Jewish Ledger." As if God's will was at work, my lifelong friend, Lusia Wajntraub-Hack, sent me the article not knowing what it would bring to my life. Lusia had no way of knowing that she had sent me the last missing piece of the puzzle.

I realized that God works in mysterious ways. It all came to me like a flash of lightning. I had to be in places halfway around the world and meet people that came my way, not realizing they were God's helpers and were instrumental for my search to finally come to a successful end.

Was all the suffering worth it? Yes! Yes! Yes!

As I wrote to Adam in one of my letters, "I don't know what kind of person you became and even if you are a criminal, I may not approve of your deeds, but to me you are my brother."

After our birthday celebration, the Kalukins invited us to the fiftieth anniversary of the liberation of Stutthof, the women's death camp. As usual, the *Gdanska Televisja* TV crew followed us with their van. Perhaps because of this publicity, wherever we went, we were treated as honored guests.

On the way to Stutthof, we were following the TV crew's van, when suddenly Adam's car blew a tire. We had purchased the tire the day before at a car stockyard. It was a used one, which apparently had been repainted, and we were fooled. Adam immediately went to the nearest farmhouse to seek help since gas stations were scarce on the roads we were traveling. We found a young man who promised to fix the tire by the time we returned. The TV crew, noticing that we were not following them, backtracked to find us waiting by the road. We continued our journey with them.

Getting closer to the concentration camp, I became very agitated. I could not face the actual place of mass murder. After the war, I avoided going on any trips to death camps. I was not alone with these feelings. Most survivors living in Poland avoided visiting the tragic places where the Jewish people were slaughtered. Even when I returned on two occasions to Poland, I still was not able to make this pilgrimage. But now, with Adam at my side, and with the TV crew looking over our shoulders, I found the strength, knowing that our visit would bring attention to the Polish audiences and future generations of what happened to the Jewish people here.

© *Szymon Kaczmarczyk/shutterstock.com*

It was a startling sunny day. It was a great ordeal to approach the gates and enter. But seeing the gas chambers and crematoria made me shiver, and I was in a panic. I was tormented to see where many thousands of our brave people, young and old— babies - took their last steps to an unimaginable brutal death.

Soon, thousands of people started to arrive, forming a body of marchers. We met Holocaust survivors from Ukraine, Latvia, and Russia. The gathered humanity came for the same purpose— to walk the path their loved ones walked before they were murdered with brutality.

On a raised platform, government officials and clergy offered prayers and speeches only for Poles. No rabbi spoke on behalf of the Jews. The only acknowledgment that was offered over the loudspeaker before the official speeches was a reading of names of the murdered. They were identified as *Zydowka - Zyd,* (a Jewess, a Jew).

Emotionally and physically exhausted, we returned to pick up the car, which was fixed with a temporary patch. We were able to return to Wejcherowo.

By this time, Adam urged that I remain longer in Poland. He teased, "After fifty-three years of being separated, you want to go home after visiting for only two weeks?"

I understood what he was saying, but would his wife agree to my extending the visit? I asked him to discuss it with his wife. When the answer was yes, I changed my return plans.

The next plan was a trip to Sosnowiec to get Adam's birth certificate. We hoped it would be ready, since I requested it months before I came. At the city hall registry of birth and death certificates, we were greeted by three friendly women. After a long wait, we were informed that there was no birth certificate under his name. I disputed that Adam was my twin brother, and if I had a birth certificate, so did, he. I started to cry after I was informed that my certificate was prepared after the war in 1949.

"It can't be," I sobbed.

I commented out loud, "So Father never made one for Adam.

How fast Father gave up on Adam."

I wanted to know what was in the archives, and where my sister Gienia's birth certificate was. The clerk made another search for Gienia's birth certificate, but all she found was a notation on Gienia Paluch, who was not our sister but a cousin also named Gienia who was born in 1937. She was the daughter of our father's younger brother, Gedalie. Both his wife and only child were murdered in Auschwitz.

The clerks sympathized with my frustration and sorrow and promised that they would make a special effort to find whatever they could in the next few days.

When we returned to the registrar's office again, we were told, "We looked all over but the only thing we found is..." she stopped speaking as she hesitatingly looked at my determined face and my resolve to learn anything and everything. She continued, "Do you know how your mother died?"

I replied, "Yes, I knew."

She handed me the paper she was holding and told me, "This is your mother's death certificate, the only one we have from those times. " Adam and I stared at the certificate with disbelief. There it was, her name, her birth date, her death date, and even the hour of her death, 12:00 p.m. It had the address where she jumped to her death and even her address during our stay in the ghetto. It was in German and signed by a German policeman.

It stated the cause of death was suicide. I felt as if my whole being was in a state of shock. Coming to myself, we decided to go to the place where it happened. It seemed we were reliving a nightmare that we had forgotten.

With the death certificate information in hand and wanting to explore our lives, we arrived in Pogon the next day. This was the location of our home before we were taken to the ghetto.

We were in a traumatized condition when we searched out the actual address that was in the archives—the building where we lived. The building wasn't anywhere to be found. We knocked on doors to try and find people who might have remembered our family. We came to a green shack-like structure and knocked on the door and window, but no one responded. We stopped people on the street and asked if they knew what happened to the street during the war. They gave us some names and pointed to buildings that might have older people who might remember.

After many disappointments, we came to the home of Mr. Jureczko, who told us he remembered our father. He had tailored his first two suits, one for his communion and the other for a vacation in Krynica when was a teenager. He led us to the place where our home stood and explained that it was removed to make room for the trams. Across the street stood a church. I was convinced that this was the place. Father did tell me that our house was located across from a church.

Mr. Jureczko invited us to his house and agreed to give us a notarized statement that he knew our family and knew they had a

Nr. 394

Sosnowitz, den 20. August 1942

Die Estera Sara Palnek

Sosnowiec 1935, 05, 29, ___, jüdisch

wohnhaft in Sosnowitz, Modhorgasse 23

ist am 14. August 1942 ___ um ___ 12 Uhr ___ Minuten

in Sosnowitz, Marktstrasse 8 ___ verstorben.

Die Verstorbene war geboren am 13 April 1906

in Szczekociny

(Standesamt ___ Nr. ___)

Vater: unbekannt

Mutter: unbekannt

Die Verstorbene war — nicht — verheiratet

Eingetragen auf mündliche — schriftliche — Anzeige der Staatlich.

Kriminalpolizei in Sosnowitz

D ___ Anzeigende

Vorgelesen, genehmigt und ___ unterschrieben

Der Standesbeamte

In Vertretung: A. Wilhelm

Todesursache: Selbstmord durch Sprung aus dem Fenster
vom 2. Stockwerk des Hauses Sosnowitz, Marktstrasse 8

Eheschließung de ___ Verstorbenen am ___ in ___

Our mother's death certificate

boy and girl, twins, and an older sister, but he could not recall the names.

We returned to Sosnowiec with the television crew who took videos of Mr. Jureczko showing us where our home stood. We also found other people who remembered the Jewish tailor, his wife, and children. As we walked around our neighborhood, I felt as if we were back in time, visualizing our own mother walking down the street, proudly pushing her twins in a stroller. It was a feeling that I wanted to continue so that I could recapture the lost, tender times that seemed to possess me now.

Our search was confirmed when we discovered the landlady's daughter, who remembered us well as babies. She even told me that she had asked our mother, "What do you feed your twins? They look so chubby." She told us that Mother replied with satisfaction, "I feed them cream of wheat cereal and milk."

Every bit of information felt like I was being enriched with a new spirit which embraced my soul. Adam, too, was mesmerized to learn so much about his past.

We returned to Częstochowa, where we stayed with Lidia. The next day, we went back to Wejcherowo. We also made plans to go to Zakopane, and this time Adam's wife joined us. We planned that on the way to Zakopane, we would stop in Sosnowiec. I needed to prove to myself that my nightmare and the chaos of chasing Mother was a real memory. Here was the three-dimensional space that I could visualize and this time understand the tragedy that befell me and my siblings at such tender years.

I asked Adam and his wife to join me in retracing the steps that I remembered, step by step. I described the appearance of the inside of the building from the point of view of a three and a half-year-old toddler. I described the entrance and the stairway to the left. On the second floor, I described a closet. And it was there, although at this time it was boarded and painted over—it was used in the interior of the adjoining apartment. Another flight of stairs and a window was exactly as I remembered.

I looked at my brother, but there was no recollection on his face. We looked out the window where I saw Mother lay lifeless below. At that time, I did not understand the horror. No words were exchanged between us.

When we were leaving the building, I felt very distraught and almost angry that Adam could not retrieve a memory of that day. I was ready to scream at him, but all I was able to do is shake him and say, "Don't you remember your mother, the woman with a crown of braided hair?"

Apologizing for his lack of memory, Adam looked at his wife and she at him and answered, "When I met my wife, that's how she looked— the way you have described our mother." She nodded her head yes.

We left the scene with a final goodbye to our mother's spirit and continued to Zakopane where the Holocaust Child Survivors were meeting. Adam was greeted warmly by everyone who had arrived before us. He paraded me around, introducing me with a sense of pride and announcing this miraculous happening. His lifelong search for his identity was over. He now knew who he was and had found his twin. His face was aglow with a blush and a glint in his eyes. Many there teared up with both gladness and sadness of their own personal, unresolved losses.

Thinking that his wife may feel left out, we tried to include her in everything that was going on around us, especially when the Gdansk TV arrived to video us during the gathering. They took us, with their van, to the most beautiful site in Zakopane, *Morskie Oko*, (Sea Eye Lake). Later, with a special jeep, we were driven up the mountain where only special vehicles were allowed in an attempt to diminish the pollution in this area.

The weather was beautiful and the view breathtaking. The mountains looked magical and majestic against the background of the early morning pink sky. The water in the lake was clear and cold. The snow still remaining on the Karpaty Mountains was slowly melting and streaming into the lake at this location. Here, the TV crew listened as Adam and I shared our stories about our endless searches. At times, the camera switched to Adam's wife to capture her reactions.

When we were brought back to the hotel of the gathered child survivors, close to two hundred people were seated at long tables inside the huge dining room. The TV crew asked permission to videotape the happening, but the participants did not want to be taped. They still feared being identified as Jews by their own families, friends, and neighbors, or feared losing their jobs.

At the end of the dinner, Mrs. Bieta Ficowska spoke. She told the gathered about Adam and me and asked people to join in the celebration of our reunion at a fireside party outside the hotel.

The television crew decided to interview Adam's foster parents in their apartment in Lebork. The entire morning, Adam's foster mother prepared food and drinks for all of us. When her husband invited Adam and me to stand up, he said he wanted to tell us something important. I was sure that it was going to be a toast, but instead he said, "I have a solution for you. All Jews should be moved to Madagascar."

During the war, it was proposed that all Jews should be relocated there. I felt like a bullet went through my head. All that I managed to say was, "This is 1995, and the time you send Jews away are gone. I don't have to take this conduct or attitude anymore!"

I left the room slamming the door as hard as I could. Only when I was outside did my tears flood my eyes. Adam was the only one who came to offer comfort. The rest did not bother to support me; not even the TV crew nor Adam's wife came out to console me. Adam stayed with me outside until it was time to go back to Wejherowo.

Part of the edited movie, "A Fortunate Man" was shown a year and a half later on Polish TV. It included his wife's account of what happened since her husband left for the United States. It was completely twisted, and not the same video version that was given to me, the full-length version, which they hoped to sell outside of Poland.

As Adam and I became inseparable, every opportunity that his wife was alone with me, she would badmouth him. She started to portray him as a man who was mentally sick, forgetful, a womanizer— one who had no understanding how to take care of his family. Every evening Adam was attacked by his screaming wife and sons. Their financial demands were great, and in spite of him making a decent living working part time, plus his combatant's pension, the rent from his real estate, as well as all the other money, was going straight into his wife's hands.

Adam told me that he wanted to go with me to the United States to get to know the family. The closer it got to my departure, the more Adam begged to take him with me.

One day Adam told me, "You see for yourself how my own family treats me with contempt. Please take me out of Poland, even if it is for a short time. This land has become a Jewish cemetery."

Every day, the atmosphere grew more tense in Adam's home. I arranged a visa for Adam through the American Embassy to come with me at the end of May. We bought a ticket for Adam, which I guarded and kept on me at all times, together with his passport.

We revisited Sosnowiec where we searched out the Jewish cemetery, which was vandalized many times. The gravestones were missing, and skulls and bones were strewn about as the locals dug up the graves, still looking for gold filling in the Jewish teeth. It was a nightmare to try to find our mother's grave.

Seeing the shambles of this holy place, Adam was determined to bring the Gdansk TV crew to tape it in order to record these shocking conditions. They did come and spent a lot of time taping the cemetery's sorrowful state, but this part of the tape did not appear in their movie— the version for the Polish audience. As we discovered later, it was only in the version that was sent to us to be shown in the United States.

After leaving this country, knowing that we did not have any family in Poland, I informed Adam that I was not his only relative. There were cousins living on different continents. Tova and Jona, daughters of our father's youngest brother, Gedalie, who lived in Israel. Sadly, Uncle Gedalie passed away a few years ago. We also had cousins in Brazil, Basia, the daughter of our mother's sister Aunt Sabina. She was left alone after her mother was shot on the streets of Gdynia when it was discovered that she was a Jew. Sabina took on an identity as a Pole and lived with her Catholic boyfriend's parents. Two other cousins, the children of Mother's brother Shmulik, emigrated from Russia first to Poland and then to Brazil.

The television crew came to our departure at the Gdansk airport. All the footage that was taken of Adam and me during our reunion was produced by Mr. Kalukin into a film which we learned was made into two versions. One for Poland and the other for the Western audiences. He told us that this movie won a first prize in a festival of international films. I'm sure that the prize was awarded for the version where the truth was presented, unbiased. The prize was given for truth, but the truth was cut to pieces out of the version shown at the Polish Film Festival. I was outraged that our lives were used to appease and support the anti-Semitic views still heldbymanyinPoland.

I couldn't wait to get on the first plane to Warsaw and home to the United States. We arrived at O'Hare Airport on May 31, 1995. Quickly, we went through customs, and Sam greeted us at the exit. He was relieved to have me return home safely, but he was nervously observing the stranger, my twin brother, Adam.

Because Adam did not speak English, I was his translator trying to maintain a conversation with my husband, as I defended my decision to bring Adam with me. I told Sam that when the opportunity arose, I had to bring him home to meet the family.

As we passed the streets of Chicago, especially Milwaukee Avenue, I told Adam about the large Polish population that live in and around Milwaukee Avenue, equal to the Jackowo neighborhood in Poland.

Actually, Chicago has the largest Polish population in the world next to Warsaw. Here, most of the stores have Polish signs and one hears Polish spoken in all dialects. The only difference is that those delicatessen stores are better supplied with Polish sausage, ham, and baked goods than in Poland. The Polish bookstores carry the most popular and recent books, newspapers, magazines, and recordings.

Then we passed to the Edgewater neighborhood and the suburb of Skokie where we live. There were many messages from friends and strangers in response to the Chicago Tribune, May, 31 1995 front page heading, *"Holocaust twins find one another, after fifty-three years apart. Skokie woman's search for brother ends happily."* The story was accompanied by a photograph of Mother holding us, the twins, on her lap.

I was brought to tears when I saw that our older sister Gienia's face was cut out. I regretted a missed opportunity to let the world know that Adam and I are still determined to find her because, without her, we are still not complete.

Adam shared our home in his own private quarters, in the lower level of our ranch, where a separate bedroom and bath gave him privacy. Soon after arriving, we went shopping for his immediate needs, since Adam brought very little clothing from home. Now we were recognized in restaurants and on the streets as the miracle twins who found each other after a fifty-three-year search.

The following day, we were invited by the Holocaust Museum Foundation to share our story in the Skokie Veterans Hall. We met the Skokie Mayor, Jacqueline Gorell, and had pictures taken with her and Erna Gans, the president of the Holocaust Foundation. There were many local school children and parents in the audience.

We spoke about our emotional, miraculous reunion in Poland and were received with welcoming applause by all. Lawyers, who were present there, promised to help get Adam's identity back as Adam Paluch in the U.S. court system.

The first phone calls that Adam made to Poland to his family were not well-received at the other end. Sometimes, his wife wouldn't come to the telephone. The sons, too, wouldn't talk to their father. The only conversation I recall is when his wife asked for money. Adam left all to his family.

After many years, the family finally accepted us, and I hope they finally understand the bond of sister and brother, twins, and the connection to our lost family.

In spite of Adam's age, at eighty, he is still very active and adapts to new situations quickly. Together we address students and other audiences and are proof that miracles happen. I'm so proud of Adam. He is my soulmate.

My life has been in turmoil from the age of three, not understanding the undercurrent. To finally have answers, a connection and bond to my own brother, has healed me.

My Holocaust memories are turbulent and at times unforgiving, but I have memories of people in my life who nurtured me and accepted who I am and helped me find peace.

My brother, Adam, too, has had a turbulent life, but his was one of looking for the unknown, and then he was faced with turmoil and alienation from his own family. But as the saying goes, "All is well that ends well." And so is his story. His sons and grandchildren are in touch with him, and he has found the rich, although hurtful history of his life.

My own story is a life complete. I was able to have Yad Vashem honor my dear Jozefa with an award as a Righteous. And have placed a memorial brick in loving memory of my mother, Ester, and my Polish parents, Jozefa and Wilhelm Maj.

IN LOVING MEMORY OF ESTER
PALUCH, WHO GAVE ME LIFE,
AND JOZEFA & WILHELM MAJ,
WHO SAVED MY LIFE
YOUR DEVOTED DAUGHTER,
IDA PALUCH KERSZ

בזכירה סוד הגאולה
(הבעש"ט)
W wiecznej pamięci leży
tajemnica odkupienia
(Baal-Szem-Tow)

כאילו קיים עולם מלא ❖❖ כל המקיים נפש אחת
KTO RATUJE JEDRO ❖❖ KTO RATUJE JEDRO

תעודת כבוד
Dyplom Honorowy

NINIEJSZYM ZAŚWIADCZA SIĘ, ŻE RADA D/S SPRAWIEDLIWYCH WŚRÓD NARODÓW ŚWIATA PRZY INSTYTUCIE PAMIĘCI NARODOWEJ YAD VASHEM PO ZAPOZNANIU SIĘ ZE ZŁOŻONĄ DOKUMENTACJĄ POSTANOWIŁA NA POSIEDZENIU W DNIU 22 · III · 2011 r. ODZNACZYĆ

Józefę i Wilhelma Majów

MEDALEM SPRAWIEDLIWYCH WŚRÓD NARODÓW ŚWIATA, W DOWÓD UZNANIA, ŻE Z NARAŻENIEM WŁASNEGO ŻYCIA RATOWALI ŻYDÓW PRZEŚLADOWANYCH W LATACH OKUPACJI HITLEROWSKIEJ. IMIONA ICH UWIECZNIONE BĘDĄ NA HONOROWEJ TABLICY W PARKU SPRAWIEDLIWYCH WŚRÓD NARODÓW ŚWIATA NA WZGÓRZU PAMIĘCI W JEROZOLIMIE.

וזאת לתעודה שבישיבתה
ביום ט"ז אדר ב' תשע"א
החליטה הוועדה לציון
חסידי אומות העולם
שליד רשות הזיכרון יד ושם
על יסוד עדויות
שהובאו לפניה, לתת כבוד
ויקר ל-

יוזפה וּוילהלם מאי

על אשר בשנות השואה
באירופה שמו נפשם בכפם
להצלת יהודים נרדפים
מידי רודפיהם ולהעניק להם
את המדליה לחסידי אומות
העולם.
שמם יונצח לעד על לוח-
כבוד בחורשת חסידי אומות
העולם ביד ושם.

Jerozolima, Izrael, dnia
20 · VI · 2011 r.

ניתן היום בירושלים
י"ח סיון תשע"א

AVNER SHALEV
בשם רשות הזיכרון יד ושם
W IMIENIU "YAD VASHEM"

JACOB TURKEL
בשם הועדה לציון חסידי אומות העולם
W IMIENIU RADY D/S SPRAWIEDLIWYCH

Diploma to honor my dear Jozefa with an award as a Righteous.

30

ADAM'S MEMORIES

When Adam was a grown man, visiting the concentration camp Majdanek with his sons, upon seeing the entrance, he froze. He could not enter. Memories, confused memories, overwhelmed him. Adam's memories where shut down. At about the age of five, some pieces surfaced.

Majdanek Concentration Camp was liberated by the Russian Army in July 1944. His earliest memory was of being found by Russian soldiers in a latrine at Majdanek, wrapped in a German raincoat.

He remembered being taken to a hospital where he was treated for open wounds on the right side of his head. This is where he was told that he was one of the children that the Germans experimented on. This information had no meaning. He only knew that he had no one to comfort him. He lost all sense of who he was and where he belonged. Adam believes that if the war lasted another year, he would have been dead.

After the hospital stay, Adam was taken to an orphanage that was established near the Majdanek Concentration Camp. This is where his foster parents, who had no children, went to take in a girl child but took Adam. They had him baptized, and somehow his baptismal document read that he was a girl. He learned about this when he visited the church, but the papers were not corrected. Eventually, the foster parents had six children—four boys and two girls.

As a little boy, he had light blonde hair. The woman at the store, where he went to pick up some groceries, told him that he was a

Zhydowski child (Jewish child) and that his stupid foster mother was dying his hair to make him look Polish. As he grew older, his hair turned dark.

Adam and his foster father

His childhood was always full of questioning, but he had no one to question. He was often bullied and beaten by the neighborhood kids. They started to call him *obrzezaniec* (circumcised), but Adam did not understand what it meant.

Being Jewish and circumcised was a problem in his boyhood friendships. When he saw a doctor, he asked if his adoptive father was a Jew. He learned what it meant. His search began. Apparently, the circumcision was a marker of being Jewish and was intriguing to a young child.

Adam never felt accepted, and was an outsider even among his Polish family. Even his foster grandmother told him that he was a foundling. Often, Adam rebelled by running away from being abused. He was beaten and never felt that he belonged. The beatings were administered by the parents and a foster uncle, a drunk shoemaker. When this uncle was tipsy, he would say to Adam that he had a *Zhydowska glowa* (Jewish head—smart) because Adam played chess very well.

On many occasions, at the age of eight, Adam ran away from home. He was found by the police and returned to his Polish family. They all thought that he was not normal and consulted a doctor. As he states now, "People don't run away from good places."

As of the third grade, around the age of ten, Adam, in earnest, started to search and question who he was. The Polish father, who was a painter, and family moved to Warsaw for a short time. One of his friends, a Jew and a tailor, told Adam that he, too, was a Jew. Adam asked him to help him learn something about himself and his family.

"Your search is hopeless. Everyone was killed," was his answer.

When Adam tried to have his Polish foster family acknowledged as "Righteous Among Nations" by Yad Vashem, Jerusalem, the truth became known. They did not save him. They took him out of a temporary orphanage near Majdanek after the war. All these lies only intensified the questions of who he was and where he belonged.

Adam knew he was different. He had different aspirations and outlooks than the Polish boys his age. When Adam excelled in his studies, his foster father would say that he had a *Yiddishe Kepele* (a Jewish head), which is sometimes used by Jewish parents to applaud the successful studies of their children.

Even after the war, being Jewish was an obstacle to acceptance and blending in. He often heard jeers directed at him, "*Zhyd*" with an undertone of anti-Semitism. When he encountered anti-Semitism, when people spoke badly against Jews, he confronted the hateful conversations.

At the age of around fourteen, during vacation time, he left home and worked at whatever job that he could and sent his earnings to the family. He thought of leaving, but he had no other place to call home.

Adam did attend a Boarding Technical High School. Afterwards, he continued at a university and studied chemistry. He aspired to become a famous chemist and accomplish great achievements. His plan was that maybe then the Jewish people would find him and be proud of him.

His quest to find his identity never stopped. From a very young age Adam tried to find who he was, his name, his Jewish identity, perhaps a family member. He went to Warsaw to the Jewish Community Office, but they could not help him because he had no identity or memory of who he was. He did not know his real name.

He had to stop his education when his adoptive father was arrested for underhanded dealing. Adam had to work full time to help the family. He was employed at the Technician Lab, working on research projects using coal mine products, testing synthetics.

Adam married his wife in 1965. After three dates, he told her that he would marry her. She was embarrassed and called him stupid. Three months later when she took him to meet her parents, the father asked how he would support her. He changed his attitude against this marriage when he learned that Adam's income was much more than his own.

By 1975 they had three sons who Adam loved and provided well for. But through the years, the relationship with his wife was strained. Part of it was the mistrust when some valuable things went missing. Two years later, she admitted that she took the valuables to her sister's house from which they were stolen.

In 1991, he heard about a Jewish child survivor gathering in Warsaw. He decided to learn what they were all about. They immediately accepted him to the organization and acknowledged his Jewish roots. They gave him hope to continue the search. Someone out there may be able to help identify him.

Almost as a final attempt of his search, a reporter from Connecticut attending the survivors' gathering took some information which she published in the States with a picture of Adam.

When Adam heard Ida's voice the first time on the phone, he was stunned and thought it was a prank. He was not that lucky to learn his real name and where he belonged after fifty-three years.

When he called Ida back in Skokie, and she told him that they may be siblings, and actually twins, his head was reeling. Her voice and her assured, confident statements, were exciting, but it was hard to believe that she had the true answer to his identity. He did not want to be disappointed again.

For three months, they corresponded and exchanged pictures, and finally Ida convinced him that they were sister and brother when she sent a letter signed, "Your sister."

After inspecting all the pictures, he, too, was convinced that they were family. He cried and was emotional with gladness and a sense of a great loss, especially since he had no memories of his toddler years.

The conclusion to this search is that Ida and Adam are now a united family. He remained in America and sadly had a difficult time being estranged from his children. But with the years and maturity of his sons, they have reconnected and are closer now. They even came to see their father in America.

In 2001, Ida went to Poland and visited her nephews and families, and she was received with warmth. Also in 2001, by court order in Poland, Adam received a birth certificate with his birth name Adam Paluch.

Adam and Ida, 2019

ABOUT THE AUTHOR

Ida Paluch Kersz has been a volunteer, speaker, and served on the board of directors of the Illinois Holocaust Museum and Education Center in Skokie for over thirty years. She has contributed countless hours sharing her survival with thousands of students and visitors at the museum and other venues.

Ida has often joked that her childhood was very similar to that of Cinderella because of the relationship she had with her stepmother and the many mornings she had to get up early and start the oven before anyone else awakened.

Ida also often had to wear shoes with holes in them as a youth. The two experiences have led to her adult obsession with shoes. She has an extensive collection of glass decorative shoes, many more than the real Cinderella.

Ida now lives in Winnetka, Illinois.

CPSIA information can be obtained
at www.ICGtesting.com
Printed in the USA
BVHW081329101122
651207BV00004B/12